PEPPER SHRIMP PAELLA, PAGE 161

Yawd

Modern Afro-Caribbean Recipes

ADRIAN FORTE

appetite
by RANDOM HOUSE

Appetite by Random House® and colophon are regis-
tered trademarks of Penguin Random House LLC.

Library and Archives Canada Cataloguing in
Publication is available upon request.

ISBN: 978-0-525-61156-1
eBook ISBN: 978-0-525-61157-8

Photography by John Molina
Book and cover design by Jennifer Griffiths
Printed and bound in China

Published in Canada by Appetite by Random House®, a
division of Penguin Random House Canada Limited

www.penguinrandomhouse.ca

10 9 8 7 6 5 4 3 2 1

appetite
by RANDOM HOUSE

This book is dedicated to the multi-ethnic Afro-Caribbean community. For many years Black chefs have felt unseen, unheard, and underrepresented in the hospitality industry, left out of the conversation, and with a lack of Black mentors and role models to look up to. This book is a testament to all the hard work our community has been doing for generations before me. I am privileged and honored to have a platform and be in a position to continue to tell our stories about our food and our people through our own lenses.

Contents

CHAPTER 5: SIDES

CHAPTER 6: VEGETABLE MAINS

CHAPTER 7: FISH & SEAFOOD

CHAPTER 8: POULTRY & MEAT

CHAPTER 9: DESSERTS

Introduction

Growing up in Kingston, Jamaica, my earliest memories all involve food. One of my fondest memories from childhood is that feeling of looking forward to the weekend—not because I would get to sleep in, watch cartoons, or eat ackee and salted cod on Saturday morning (although I did love that!), but because of Friday night. I knew on Friday night I would attend church service, and on the way home, when it was late, and we were all hungry, we would drive past the jerk chicken vendors. The smell of the spices and the smoke wafting, the sound of the music, and the sight of people gathering to eat—all dressed up before going out for the night—is ingrained in my brain, and jerk has been a fundamental part of my evolution as a chef.

Cooking was a family thing for us. My dad's mom ran a cookshop—a small, casual, almost take-out style restaurant—and my mom's mom was the go-to cook for everyone in our family, and the whole neighborhood, really. She didn't have any formal culinary training, but she was always being asked to cook for church gatherings, birthday parties, and all kinds of events. With two grandmothers who were great cooks, I came to understand the basics of cooking early on. But it was my mom's mom who taught me the most. She was the type of cook who understood food in the most fundamental way. She didn't need a recipe, a timer, or a thermometer, because she knew intuitively how to get things just right. I swear you could taste the love in her cooking. She was a machine in the kitchen—every movement was made with efficiency—but she was also natural and relaxed, and we had *fun*. In her kitchen, the music was always blasting. I loved to hang out with her there. It put me in such a zen mood.

Now, whether I'm making a recipe I know by heart or preparing the most complicated tasting menu, I always feel positive and relaxed when I'm cooking, and I know that's down to her.

My grandma started me off with simple tasks, like peeling garlic, chopping onions, and boiling and peeling eggs—and I asked *a lot* of questions. On Sundays, my job in the kitchen was to clean, tenderize, and season whatever choice of meat that was for dinner. This was a huge responsibility and I had to make sure it was perfect. Saturdays were synonymous with soup—Soup Saturday as it's known in Jamaica. The soup of the week depended on what was available at the shop (the local grocery store) and whatever ingredients we had leftover from dinners during the week. I was tasked to go shopping for the protein. My uncle would give me $250 Jamaican and tell me to "buy a pound of flour and get whatever meat you can with whatever left back." I would generally opt for chicken feet; they are my favorite, and were the most inexpensive, so I could buy tons to go around (the more premium proteins, like snapper or chuck, didn't fit the budget we were working with!). As I was heading out the door, my aunts and uncles would be getting the base of the soup ready: carrots, onions, scallions, and a bit of Scotch bonnet, plus a package or two of Grace Cock Soup (a bouillon powder of concentrated vegetable seasoning, and tiny shards of noodles). Then we'd add in different ground provisions depending on the protein in the soup, and what was in season. Chicken and beef soups would usually include yellow yam, Jamaican sweet potato, cassava, corn, sometimes plantains, and always spinners (flour dumplings); the seafood versions had many of the same, usually with chayote or okra in the mix too.

When I was about 15 or 16, I moved from Kingston to Long Island, New York. My mother had been diagnosed with pancreatic cancer and wanted to give me a better chance of succeeding, so she sent me to live with her mom, who had recently moved to New York. Those years were the most formative of my life—I learned so much about myself while living under my grandmother's roof. It's where I truly discovered my passion and love for cooking, and where I began a relationship with God. Nothing made me happier than helping my grandmother in the kitchen. She wasn't cooking for a living anymore, but putting in long hours as a personal support worker, so I always tried to have a nice meal waiting for her when she got home. I didn't have any real interest in playing video games or sports, going to the movies, or talking to girls as a teenager—it was all about cooking. And with my grandmother as my guide, I learned a lot about the possibilities cooking offers. I learned that food not only nourishes me, but it is the best way I know how to express myself to the world. It's what makes me happy and is a huge part of what defines me as a person.

> ## I'll be forever grateful to my grandmother for introducing me to what would become my career. I wouldn't be the man I am today if I wasn't a chef.

I'll be forever grateful to my grandmother for introducing me to what would become my career. I wouldn't be the man I am today if I wasn't a chef, and if she hadn't instilled the drive and ambition I needed to make it in this industry—through culinary school at George Brown College in Toronto, my first few formative years out of school, and the ups and downs of opening several businesses. As I came up in the food industry, I didn't see many Black chefs at the helms of restaurants. A huge motivator for me has been to increase the representation of Black chefs and the cuisines those chefs could represent. With my passion and my love of cooking, I realized that I could do this: I could be one of those chefs who helped open the door for more people like me, and together, supporting each other, we could celebrate our food and bring it to the forefront.

AFRO-CARIBBEAN COOKING

I pride myself on weaving all the different influences of my life into my recipes, but my Jamaican upbringing has inspired me the most, hands down. That's something I've come back to in recent years—after years of relying on the French techniques I was taught in culinary school, and using butter and cream at every turn, I've turned back to my Afro-Caribbean roots, both in ingredients and techniques. In honing my identity as an Afro-Caribbean chef, I've been exploring more about the

RUM-SOAKED CHICKEN, PAGE 181

links between the flavors, ingredients, and ways of cooking you'll find in the Caribbean, and those of the African continent. I'm still scratching the surface of what I know will be a lifetime of learning, but what's clear to me is much of how and what we cook in the Caribbean was brought to the islands by enslaved people hundreds of years ago. From the ancestral ingredients brought over on the ships in the form of seeds, to the cooking techniques and recipes passed down orally from one generation to the next. To me, actively exploring the history of the food I've grown up with, and connecting the dots for where the ingredients I cook with originated, or how the dishes I make have evolved, is a mark of respect to my ancestors. It educates me as a chef, and means I can pass on this knowledge to the next generation.

I'm constantly inspired by new ingredients and different techniques and cuisines—people I meet, places I travel, and food I taste—and love incorporating that into new dishes and ideas.

As respectful as I am of tradition, I don't always stick to the classic way of cooking Afro-Caribbean food. Often, I've found there *isn't* one right way—through conversations with family, friends, and fellow chefs ("You put coconut milk in your curry goat?"), I've realized that different cooks and communities have their own way of doing things in the kitchen. Truthfully, I also don't want to limit myself as a chef. I'm constantly inspired by new ingredients and different techniques and cuisines— people I meet, places I travel, and food I taste—and love incorporating that into new dishes and ideas. Although I often start with a version of a traditional recipe as my base, I'm always giving food my own spin, and that's what you'll find in this book. Likewise, there are Afro-Caribbean dishes you might be familiar with that you won't find a recipe for here— things like Jamaican patties (although you will find my spin, Jamaican

Tourtières, on page 80), or johnnycakes or festival, which are heavier dishes than I generally eat. These are dishes that I know are popular, but if I don't feel like I can give you a new or different take on them, I'd rather give you something completely fresh instead.

The Jamaican motto is "out of many, one people," and there are so many different backgrounds on the island that have all come together to create the most delicious food traditions. Indo-Caribbean and Chinese-Caribbean cuisines, in particular, have had a big influence on my cooking—because I enjoy them so much, I want to build those flavors into my food!—as have Afro-Caribbean cooking from other Caribbean islands beyond Jamaica. Incorporating ideas from another cuisine into your own can be a way of showing genuine admiration for it—as long as you respectfully do the research first, and put in the time. Recently, I was developing a Trinidadian Doubles recipe for a restaurant project I'm working on, and it took me on a months-long journey to rest assured I was doing it justice. My restaurant partner, who is Trinidadian, said they weren't tasting right—although they were tasting good, they weren't what he remembered from back home. The issue, it turned out, was in my flour: I was missing the lentil flour traditionally used in Doubles. Lentil flour isn't easy to get hold of outside of Trinidad and Tobago, so I ultimately ended up going with a mix of two flours—chickpea and all-purpose—that gave me a dish I was proud of for the restaurant, while still respecting the originating culture.

The recipes in this cookbook are the culmination of my experiences and reflect who I am, where I come from, and how I grew along the way.

The recipes in this cookbook come from a life spent cooking, experimenting, learning, testing, reading, researching, and then cooking some more. They are the culmination of my experiences and reflect who I am, where I come from, and how I grew along the way. Every recipe in this book has a story behind it—whether it's from peeling potatoes in my grandmother's kitchen, bringing jerk chicken to Toronto's Little Italy (I liked to say the only thing missing was the sand), prepping hundreds of pounds of wings in a basement under a basketball arena, running a food truck without a license (but with chicken so good, the police told me how to break the law to keep it going!), or a conversation with my fellow chefs about bringing an ancestral ingredient into the spotlight—these recipes reflect what inspires me, how I like to cook, and—most importantly—what I like to eat!

With this cookbook, I hope to inspire you to cook and eat more Afro-Caribbean cuisine, and to help bring an increased appreciation and respect for it, too. I'm a huge champion for being adventurous in the kitchen, and there should be nothing holding you back from jumping into these recipes. I'm all about making food that people just *really* want to eat, because it's so damn tasty! For me, there is nothing nearly as satisfying as serving someone a heaping plate of food bursting with color and flavor, and seeing them enjoy every last bite. That's what I hope I can bring you with this book—tasty, modern, Afro-Caribbean comfort food—food that will stick to your ribs, and make you and all those you cook for smile (then ask for more).

Deliciously Yours,
Adrian Forte

Ingredients

For the recipes in this cookbook, you should be able to find all the ingredients you'll need at your local grocery store or specialty Caribbean shop. There are certain spices, herbs, and fruits and vegetables that are commonly used in Afro-Caribbean cuisine that you should know about before you start cooking, and some of them you might not have heard of before. I incorporate these ingredients into my recipes as much as possible because they're delicious and because I like to shine a spotlight on them and show people how versatile they can be. There are a few others, like breadfruit, that I love to cook with when I'm back in Jamaica, but they just aren't available enough in North America to include them in the recipes in this book and keep it as accessible as I want. Here's a quick rundown before we dive in.

Ackee

Ackee is a truly Afro-Caribbean ingredient. It's originally from Ghana, but it wasn't really used in cooking until enslaved people brought it to the Caribbean. Ackee is a fruit that bears three soft yellow pulp lobes with three black seeds surrounded by a hard red shell, when ripe (it's what I'm holding in the photo opposite the Introduction on page 1). The fruit was not consumed outside of Jamaica for many years because the unripe pulp can be poisonous! Fresh ackee is hard to come by in North America due to trade restrictions, so I call for canned; a can of ackee can range anywhere from $9 to $13 depending on the brand. Ackee makes up half of Jamaica's national dish—ackee and saltfish (see my Ackee and Saltfish Fritters, page 64).

Allspice

This ingredient is in a lot of classic Afro-Caribbean dishes, and it's the key component that gives jerk marinade and dry rub its unique flavor. Allspice is created from dried and ground pimento berries, and it gets its name because its taste is like a combination of nutmeg, cinnamon, black pepper, and cloves.

Callaloo

Callaloo (sometimes kallaloo) is a popular Caribbean dish originating in West Africa and served in different variations all across the Caribbean. It's also a green leafy vegetable, also known as amaranth, that is similar to spinach but has a stronger flavor. Callaloo can be hard to find, but you should be able to get it canned or frozen from your local Caribbean grocery store.

Cassava

This is definitely the underdog of the tuber root vegetable family (read more about them on page 13). It is a lot sweeter, creamier, and denser than its counterparts and is an extremely versatile ingredient that can be used in soups and stews or served mashed. Grounded with coconut milk and salt, it can be made into a Jamaican flatbread dough that is then fried and known as bammy (which is typically eaten with seafood). For a sweet application, the same dough can be combined with shredded coconut, condensed milk, raisins, cinnamon, and nutmeg, then baked to create a super-sticky and sweet cake called a pone.

Cinnamon

Cinnamon is an essential part of Caribbean cuisine—and is now culti- vated (and highly popular) in the region. Cinnamon can enhance both sweet and savory dishes with its robust flavor.

Cloves

Cloves play a key role in developing a good jerk marinade. They're also used in all sorts of soups, porridges, puddings, and cakes, including rum cake. But their most notable use is to help flavor the simmering liquid used to steep hibiscus flowers and make rum punch. They also remind me of Christmas and smoked ham.

Coconut

This is hands down one of the most versatile ingredients, and my all-time favorite. Each coconut product serves a specific purpose. Coconut oil can be substituted for any neutral oil used in marinades or dressings, or used as the fat for your cooking (and you'll see in the recipes it's my go-to for this). Full-fat coconut milk's thick and creamy texture and sweet flavor make it a perfect substitute for dairy-based milk in recipes like curries, soups, hot chocolates, baked goods, ice cream, smoothies, or coconut rice—basically, you name it! Coconut cream is also very versatile and can be used in a bunch of different applications, including a crowd-pleasing coconut whipped cream.

Cornmeal

Cornmeal is coarser than flour and most similar to American grits, but a little finer, and was handed down to us from our African ancestors. It can be cooked down to create a thick porridge for breakfast, or cooled and served like polenta. In Jamaica it's called tun cawnmeal, and in Barbados, cou cou. Both islands like to cook it down with chicken grease, aromatics, and okra and serve it as a side dish. In Trinidad they bake it with corn kernels and cheese and call it corn pie (see my version of this on page 115).

Garlic

I like to think of garlic as a flavor enhancer for almost everything, with its herbaceous yet mild allium taste. I make it into a garlic paste (page 24) that crops up again and again in the recipes. Add it to salad dressings and vinaigrettes or to marinades for meats and other proteins, or use it to cut the fat in rich sauces or to brighten up vegetables, soups, and stews.

Ginger

Ginger is used in many cuisines all over the world, and even though it's not native to the Caribbean, the tropical climate here offers the perfect conditions for growing it.

Ground Provisions (Tubers)

Ground provisions (also known as tubers) are vegetables that grow underground on the root of a plant. There is an assortment of tubers in the Afro-Caribbean diet: Jamaican sweet potato, yellow yam (Guinea yam), white yam (camote), dasheen (taro root), and cassava (see page 12). Ground provisions are typically boiled with herbs and spices, and served as a side dish with stews; or cubed and added to soups and other dishes.

Nutmeg

Nutmeg is often used in tandem with cloves and added to sauces, porridges, desserts, and rum punch. A pinch of nutmeg can balance out the saltiness of a savory dish or the oversweetness of any dish.

Okra

This is a very popular vegetable in a variety of Caribbean, Southern American, Indian, Asian, and South American cuisines. It can be fried, braised, baked, boiled, steamed, or stewed. Okra is a vital ingredient to Afro-Caribbean cuisine, brought to the islands by enslaved people, but is still a truly unsung hero. Just like ackee, there's a certain level of knowledge required to prepare it properly, but when done right, it's out of this world. I've used okra in sauces, stuffings, and to make chips; I've pickled it, fried it, and used the sticky enzymes as a binder agent in a variety of recipes. I've recently seen a lot of chefs of color embracing the mighty okra and hope it will soon have its moment in the spotlight. I feel proud to serve okra because of its connection to my culinary heritage, and because it's a sign of my knowledge as a chef that I can cook it well! A lot of people don't like okra because they don't know how to cook it or have had a bad experience with it, but I'm hoping my recipes will change that for you.

Oxtail

Oxtail is generally prepared by braising it with aromatics, water, and bouillon powder. Specific preparations vary by community, but the end result is always the same: tender-to-the-bone morsels of meat, packed with umami beef flavor, and a velvety-smooth sauce created from the secretion of marrow from the bone during the braising process. Oxtail is great for soups and stews, and adds a nice unctuousness to any meal.

Paprika

Paprika is made by grinding up dehydrated bell and chili peppers, and in Afro-Caribbean cooking the most common varieties used are smoked and sweet paprika. Paprika can be used to marinate proteins, as a smoky element in sauces, as a replacement for spicy peppers, or as a garnish to add a red hue or tint to finished dishes. It's also key to the West African chicken seasoning blend called suya.

Plantains

When it comes to staple ingredients in Afro-Caribbean cuisine, plantains are at the top of the food chain. Green plantains can be used to make chips or tostones, and ripe, or yellow plantains can be boiled, mashed, or deep-fried and incorporated into savory dishes and desserts.

Salt

Salts come in a variety of sizes, flavors, and colors from all over the world: pink Himalayan, gray, black Hawaiian, flaked, smoked, coarse, fine, kosher, table. Kosher is my personal salt of choice and the one I default to in these recipes. It's a flaked salt that contains fewer additives and has a cleaner and more even taste than ordinary table salt. When used in cooking, kosher salt flakes dissolve more easily, and due to the shape and size of the granules, there's actually less salt in a pinch of kosher salt than in ordinary table salt.

Salted Cod

Salted cod, or saltfish, is a dried, salted fish that you buy packaged and then rehydrate by soaking it in water. It was originally introduced by the British, who needed rations at sea that would last as long as possible. Then, during the early days of the transatlantic slave trade, sugar plantation owners would import it as an inexpensive way to feed the enslaved people. It has a complicated history, but it's now a popular ingredient that is used in many dishes—and not least as one half of Jamaica's national dish, ackee and saltfish.

Scotch Bonnets

The Scotch bonnet is one of the hottest peppers in the world, packed with robust sweet flavor and an underlying heat, ranking right up there with the habanero. It's most famously used in jerk marinades and pepper sauces, as well as to season meat, fish, and poultry dishes that require a nice kick of spice. It can be added minced, chopped, or whole, and you can reduce a lot of the heat from the peppers by removing the seeds or pickling them (as on page 20).

Essentials

JERK

The term "jerk" refers to the technique of smoking an ingredient over pimento wood, and not necessarily the marinade or seasoning used. If you're smoking an ingredient with pimento wood and charcoal, you have jerk! A jerk dry rub is usually applied to the protein before it is smoked to set the base layer of flavor before the protein is basted with a jerk marinade. That sweet, tangy, and spicy marinade we know now as jerk was actually invented by the Taíno, an Indigenous people of the Caribbean, and used as a way to preserve meat.

In high school in Jamaica, every kid learns about our seven National Heroes. Some of them are better known outside of Jamaica, but the one who has always meant the most to me is Nanny of the Maroons. Not only is she Jamaica's only female national hero, but she was responsible for the freedom of large numbers of enslaved people—battling against the British, after escaping from a boat herself, before it had docked on the island. As a legendary figure, there are different stories about Nanny, but this is what I often heard growing up. Nanny and her soldiers camped in the mountains, where they formed their own community with the Taíno. They didn't want the British to find their campsites, so they built fires in holes in the ground. Marinated wild pigs would be placed on wood, which was placed over the fire, and then the area would be re-covered to stop the smoke from being seen. The meat would slow cook over low temperature. The meat's marinade, and this low and slow cooking process, has evolved into what we know as jerk today. It's in a tradition that has been kept alive for hundreds of years, and become one of Jamaica's most famous exports.

I developed my own jerk recipes in 2011, when I was working for a Caribbean catering company in Toronto. There I spent hours of my life honing and crafting skills that I didn't know would be an integral part of my development, not just as a chef but as a human being. We were known for selling these delicious boneless jerk chicken sandwiches on coco bread with creamy coleslaw. If you went to any event, nightclub, or get-together in Toronto and these sandwiches weren't there, your party wasn't popping!! Being the new kid in the kitchen, I had the responsibility of deboning, butchering, cleaning, and then seasoning all the chicken thighs. Up until this point I had only ever used store-bought jerk seasoning and marinades for my cooking. We booked a client for a reception of 5,000 people, and I saw it as my opportunity to create my own version of jerk—and have thousands of people try it! I told my boss I wanted to make my own jerk seasoning, then took everything I knew about jerk and the ingredients I had on hand, and hoped for the best. My jerk was a hit, and from there, there was no looking back—culminating in me opening my own restaurant in Little Italy, AF1 Caribbean Canteen.

With AF1 I wanted to give people a truly authentic jerk experience, with meat smoked slow and low over pimento wood for hours to get that smoky pimento taste to the bone. It nearly bankrupted me. I learned the hard way that importing pimento wood to Canada from Jamaica was not going to be financially or practically sustainable, but it was so important to me because of the history of how jerk first came to be.

Due to import restrictions, and the scarcity of pimento wood, the easiest way to recreate jerk anything at home is to use a homemade jerk seasonings and/or marinades, and you'll see the recipes on the page opposite used time and again in this book.

JERK DRY RUB

The key to good jerk flavor is the dry rub. Whether you're sprinkling it over french fries, adding a dash to your chili, or crusting some white fish before it hits the grill, this is your base and the key first step.

MAKES: 1 CUP   **PREP: 5 MIN**   **COOK: N/A**

1 tbsp dried chives
1 tbsp onion powder
1 tbsp garlic powder
1 tbsp dried thyme
1 tbsp dried oregano
1 tbsp brown sugar
1 tbsp ground cumin
1 tbsp smoked paprika
1½ tsp ground allspice
1½ tsp ground cloves
1 tsp ground nutmeg
1 tbsp cayenne
1 tbsp crushed red pepper flakes
1½ tsp freshly ground black pepper
½ tsp salt

1. In a stainless-steel bowl, combine all the ingredients and whisk well until evenly incorporated. Store in an airtight container for up to 3 days.

JERK MARINADE

I've spent years perfecting this marinade, and I have used it in, or put it on, almost everything. I hope this brings a little taste of Jamaica, and a love of jerk, to your kitchen.

MAKES: 4 CUPS   **PREP: 5 MIN**   **COOK: N/A**

3 scallions, chopped
3 Scotch bonnet peppers
½ cup Garlic Paste (page 24)
2 cups chopped onions
2 tbsp cane sugar
2 tbsp dark rum
¼ cup fresh lime juice
½ cup puréed fresh ginger
1 tbsp ground thyme
2 tsp ground allspice
½ tsp ground cinnamon
¾ tsp grated fresh nutmeg
2 tsp freshly ground black pepper
1 tsp mushroom soy sauce
3 tbsp canola oil
1½ tbsp salt

1. Combine all the marinade ingredients in a blender and pulse until smooth and emulsified. Store in an airtight container in the fridge for up to 7 days.

PICKLED SCOTCH BONNETS

1 cup apple cider vinegar

1 tbsp pickling salt or kosher salt

½ tsp crushed red pepper flakes

4 cloves garlic, smashed

2 tsp dill seeds

3 cups Scotch bonnet peppers

Contrary to what you may think, pickling Scotch bonnets actually reduces their heat. The longer they are pickled, the less heat they have, until eventually they just taste like normal peppers. What's great about this is that you can use them at the heat level you're most comfortable with. But watch out—the heat that leaves the peppers is absorbed by the vinegar, so the longer they stay in there, the hotter the vinegar liquid gets.

MAKES: 3 CUPS   PREP: 5 MIN   COOK: 5 MIN

1. In a saucepan over medium heat, combine 1 cup water with the vinegar, salt, pepper flakes, garlic, and dill seeds and bring to a boil.

2. Place the Scotch bonnets in a sterilized 16 oz mason jar. Pour the brine over the Scotch bonnets, filling the jar to within ½ inch of the top. Seal with the lid and store for up to 3 months. Once opened, use within 6 weeks.

SCOTCH BONNET OIL

2 cups cold pressed olive oil

3 Scotch bonnet peppers, sliced in half

1 tsp smoked paprika

Salt, to taste

This spicy oil can perk up literally any dish. I like to drizzle it on fresh cucumbers with a little salt and pepper, mix it in mayonnaise or aioli, or drizzle it on pizza or meat. Use it anywhere you would normally use chili oil.

MAKES: 3 CUPS   PREP: 5 MIN   COOK: 40 MIN

1. In a medium saucepan over low heat, combine the olive oil, peppers, and paprika. Heat gently for about 40 minutes to infuse the oil with flavor; you do not want the oil to bubble or the peppers to burn. Remove from heat and allow to cool.

2. Strain the oil into a bowl, straining out the peppers and most of the paprika (some of it will probably pass through the sieve). Season with salt to taste and transfer to a cool, sterilized jar. Seal with the lid and store in the fridge for up to 6 months.

SCOTCH BONNET PASTE

I love this paste and always have some on hand. I call it my utility paste and put a little dollop in almost anything (like chili, lasagna, rice, or a marinade or dressing). Think of it as a condiment like sambal oelek; you can use it everywhere (and I do).

MAKES: ½ CUP   PREP: 2 MIN   COOK: N/A

10 Pickled Scotch Bonnets (page 20), chopped

1 large white onion, chopped

1 small carrot, chopped

5 cloves garlic, minced

½ cup apple cider vinegar

1 tbsp smoked paprika

1. Combine all the ingredients in a blender or food processor. Purée until the paste is smooth and lump-free. Transfer to a sterilized jar, seal, and store in the fridge for up to 2 weeks.

CURRY PASTE

Afro-Caribbean curries are heavily influenced by African curries and come in dry paste form, just like this one. I like to think of this paste as a time-saving tool, great to have on hand and ready to use anytime. Once it's made, all you have to do is toss it in the pan with your ingredients and you're good to go. It adds tons of flavor to a dish.

MAKES: 2 CUPS   PREP: 10 MIN   COOK: 8 MIN

1 tbsp coconut oil

4 large onions, chopped

⅓ cup Garlic Paste (page 24)

⅓ cup minced fresh ginger

⅓ cup chopped scallions

3 tbsp lemongrass paste

3 tbsp ground turmeric

3 tbsp curry powder

2 tsp ground coriander

1½ tsp salt

2 tbsp Scotch Bonnet Paste (above)

Juice of 1 lemon

¼ cup packed fresh cilantro, chopped

1. Heat the coconut oil in a skillet over medium-high heat. Add the onions, garlic paste, ginger, scallions, lemongrass paste, spices, and salt. Stir well and cook until the onions are tender, about 8 minutes.

2. Transfer to a food processor and add the Scotch bonnet paste, lemon juice, and cilantro. Pulse or purée until the paste reaches a smooth consistency. Transfer to an airtight container and store in the fridge for up to 2 weeks.

COOKING OVER FIRE

My family was often cooking over a fire in the backyard. My grandmother didn't want our house smelling like fish, so every time we made escovitch fish, we had to take the cooking to the backyard. At the time, I felt put out by the inconvenience, but I can say now that it contributed greatly to my lifelong love of cooking over an open fire. For me, there's no more satisfying way to cook. It takes immense skill and know-how, requires excellent attention to detail, and a lot of patience.

I remember my first time cooking with real fire like it was yesterday. I had just finished playing cricket with a bunch of my schoolmates, and we were all hungry. We pooled the money we had and bought some rice, chicken, and seasoning. We decided to run a boat—the Jamaican term for cooking a meal where each person brings ingredients. There's one captain (usually the best cook) who will run the boat. On that day, I was the captain, so, naturally, the boat took place in my backyard. I loaded up two rusty old car rims with charcoal, drizzled them with kerosene, dropped a matchstick in, and voilà, we had fire!

I had two Dutch ovens going at the same time. There was a pot for coconut rice and another for brown stew chicken. The pot with the chicken was releasing an amazing smell of onions caramelizing in chicken fat, which was irresistible when mixed with the smell of the fire. I didn't know much about cooking at this point, so it was all I could do to stop the stew from boiling over and putting out the fire. In the end, the meal was perfect. The chicken stew was like the most luxurious gravy. The rice had a slightly smoky aroma and crispiness from being a little too close to the fire. It probably would've been much easier if I'd cooked it over the stove, but it wouldn't have been half as fun or delicious.

GARUM FISH SAUCE

During the first wave of the COVID-19 pandemic I ordered 10 cookbooks. While everyone else was baking, I tasked myself with mastering new cooking techniques. With *The Noma Guide to Fermentation* as my bible, and an empty cupboard as my cellar, I embarked on a new culinary journey. My first stop was this sauce. Garum—originally made in Roman days by letting fish ferment in the heat of the Mediterranean sun—paved the way for today's fish sauces. You can now easily buy fish sauce at any grocery store or specialty shop, but you should try making your own; it's easy to prepare and takes only an hour or so. Do not be put off by the mess and smell during cooking; the finished garum does not smell overly fishy, but during the cooking process your kitchen will! You'll see this sauce used in multiple recipes throughout the book; it adds a nice salty, umami kick to any dish. Use it in small quantities, though, as it can get overpowering very easily.

MAKES: 1 CUP   PREP: 15 MIN   COOK: 40 MIN

1. Rinse the fish under running water, leaving them intact (do not remove the gills or innards).

2. Place the fish, salt, and herbs in a pan and add enough water to cover the fish with 1 or 2 inches of liquid on top (in my pan, that was 6 cups). Bring to a boil and let boil for 15 minutes.

3. Using a hand blender, pulse the fish to break it down completely. Continue boiling until the liquid starts to thicken, at least 20 minutes. (You can simmer the liquid longer if you like; the flavor becomes more intense the longer it cooks.) Remove from heat and let cool.

4. Use a colander to strain out any larger pieces of fish, and discard. Then strain the liquid again through a mesh strainer lined with cheesecloth until the liquid is clear. Depending on the fish used and the length of boiling time, you'll end up with a yellow to amber liquid.

5. Transfer to a sterilized jar or bottle. Store in the fridge for up to 1 year.

2 lb small fish (anchovies, smelt sprats, sardines)
2½ cups salt
2 tbsp dried oregano
2 tbsp dried mint leaves

GARLIC CONFIT

3 heads garlic, peeled
1½ cups (or more) grapeseed oil

Garlic is one of my all-time favorite ingredients to use, and applying this French confit technique transforms it into tender, sweet cloves that can enhance the flavor of any steamed, grilled, sautéed, or roasted vegetable dish, be added to compound butters, sauces, or dressings, or be used as a spread. The by-product of this garlic confit—garlic oil—is magical and can be used for searing meats, added to marinades, or used as a finishing oil on raw ingredients.

MAKES: 1 CUP   PREP: 5 MIN   COOK: 2 HR

1. Preheat the oven to 250°F.

2. Place the garlic and oil in a small baking dish (add more oil if the cloves aren't fully submerged). Cover with aluminum foil and bake until the cloves are golden and tender, about 2 hours.

3. Remove from the oven and let cool. Transfer to an airtight container and chill. Store in an airtight container (with the garlic completely covered in oil) for up to 2 weeks.

GARLIC PASTE

½ cup Garlic Confit (above)

Garlic confit paste is one of the most versatile condiments to have on hand in your pantry. Once you try this recipe, you will never go back to using the expensive little jars from your local grocer. A total game changer, this paste has the ability to completely transform any dish for the better. Generally, prepping garlic can be laborious, so having this on hand not only saves time, but makes it very easy to add garlic flavor to any dish at the last minute. Alternatively, you can create different iterations of the paste by incorporating other flavor profiles—ginger, turmeric, miso, or Parmesan—to use in curries, bisques, ramen, dressings, and pastas.

MAKES: ½ CUP   PREP: 2 MIN   COOK: N/A

1. Place the garlic confit in a blender or food processor. Purée until the paste is smooth and lump-free. Transfer to a sterilized jar, seal, and refrigerate for up to 2 weeks.

UMAMI PASTE

That strong, savory flavor you find in a lot of Asian cuisines? That is known as umami, Japanese for "yummy" or "delicious taste." I came up with a concentrated umami paste that can be used as a finishing touch in pastas, sauces, dips, and marinades or as a secret ingredient in soups, stews, chilis, and gravies.

MAKES: ½ CUP   PREP: 2 MIN   COOK: N/A

3 to 4 shiitake mushrooms, finely chopped

2 tbsp freshly grated Parmesan

2 tbsp olive oil

1 tbsp anchovy paste

1 tbsp soy sauce

1 tbsp tomato paste

1 tbsp Garlic Paste (page 24)

1 tsp Garum Fish Sauce (page 23)

½ tsp miso paste (very important)

½ tsp balsamic vinegar

Pinch of crushed red pepper flakes

1. Combine all the ingredients in a blender or food processor. Process until well blended and smooth. Taste and adjust ingredients if desired. Store in an airtight container or jar in the fridge for up to 2 weeks.

RED KIDNEY BEAN PURÉE

This recipe was inspired by the Mexican/Tex-Mex staple refried beans. After trying a Mexican lasagna in a restaurant in downtown LA, I was so impressed by how the beans were incorporated into the dish that I asked the chef for the recipe, and was inspired to give them a Caribbean twist. Plus, who doesn't like a bean purée? Put it in sandwiches, add it to soups, or use it as a dip or with my Yawdmon Burritos (page 157). Note that canned beans already have salt added to them, so I don't add salt when cooking with them. But I don't rinse them, either, to keep that saltiness intact. My grandmother had a saying that always resonated with me: "Everything in moderation, including moderation."

MAKES: 2 CUPS   PREP: 10 MIN   COOK: 15 MIN

3 tbsp olive oil (not extra virgin, as it reacts to the spices)

1 large onion, finely diced

1 (14 oz) can kidney beans with liquid

2 tbsp tomato paste

1 tbsp Garlic Paste (page 24)

½ tsp ground cumin

½ tsp ground coriander

¼ tsp ground cinnamon

1 tsp freshly ground black pepper

Zest and juice of 1 lime

1. Heat the olive oil in a skillet over medium-high heat, and sweat the onions until soft, about 7 minutes.

2. Add the beans and their liquid, and the tomato paste, garlic paste, cumin, coriander, cinnamon, and pepper. Simmer for 5 minutes. Add the lime juice, transfer to a bowl and let cool.

3. Transfer to a food processor and process until smooth, about 45 seconds. Season with additional spices to taste and transfer to a bowl. Serve warm.

GREEN SEASONING

3 bunches scallions, roughly chopped

2 banana peppers, roughly chopped

1 bunch shado beni (culantro) or fresh cilantro, roughly chopped

1 cup chopped onions

1 stalk celery, roughly chopped

1 bunch fresh thyme (about ¾ cup), roughly chopped

1 tsp salt

2 tbsp Garlic Paste (page 24)

This marinade is to Trinidadians what jerk is to Jamaicans. Herbaceous and versatile, it can be used on everything. The recipe usually calls for shado beni, also known as culantro, which isn't readily available in North America, so you can replace it with its distant cousin, cilantro. This is a great seasoning to use as a seafood or poultry marinade, or to add to dressings, soups, or stews.

MAKES: 3 CUPS   PREP: 10 MIN   COOK: N/A

1. Place all the ingredients in a blender along with ¼ cup water, and pulse.

2. With the blender turned off, use a wooden spoon to move around or push down the ingredients so everything gets worked by the blades. Continue pulsing until the marinade is the consistency of a pesto. Store in an airtight container in the fridge for up to 2 weeks.

HERB OIL

1 cup chopped scallions

1 cup fresh flat-leaf parsley

1 cup fresh basil

1 cup canola oil

You can use this oil for a variety of things: vinaigrettes, confits, marinades, fish, pasta salads, seafoods, potato salads—the list goes on! It's super versatile and you can change up the herbs in the oil and experiment with it. It's also a great alternative to a light salad dressing.

MAKES: 1 CUP   PREP: 25 MIN   COOK: 30 MIN

1. In a large bowl, place some ice and 3 cups water to create an ice bath. Set aside.

2. Bring a medium pot of water to a boil over high heat. When the water is boiling, add the scallions and parsley and cook for about 20 seconds, until they wilt and darken slightly. Drain the herbs in a strainer, then quickly transfer to the ice bath.

3. Remove the herbs from the ice bath and squeeze out as much excess water from them as possible. Transfer to a high-powered blender and add the basil. Add the oil and blend on the highest speed for 2 to 3 minutes. When you turn the blender off, the herb oil should feel warm to the touch and have a little steam rising from the top of it.

4. Set a cheesecloth-lined strainer over a bowl and pour the oil through. Don't force the oil through the strainer; just let it drain naturally into the bowl below. This may take about 30 minutes.

5. When the oil has fully drained, store in a small airtight container in the fridge for up to 3 months.

PINEAPPLE VINEGAR

Not only is this a cool way to use leftover pineapple skins, but it's one of my favorite ingredients for a tropical twist on a mignonette for oysters or to use in cocktails, salad dressings, sauces, ceviches, or any meat dish. Just use where you would any kind of vinegar.

¼ cup sugar (consider using coconut, rapadura, or panela sugar)

3 cups warm spring or filtered water

Scraps and rind of 1 pineapple

MAKES: 2 CUPS   PREP: 10 MIN + FERMENTING   COOK: N/A

1. In a sterilized 4-cup glass jar, dissolve the sugar in the water. Add the pineapple scraps and rind until the jar has ½ inch of room left at the top.

2. Cover the mouth of the jar with a square of paper towel, cheesecloth, muslin, or light fabric, and secure with a rubber band. Place in a dark cupboard or pantry and allow to ferment for 2 to 3 weeks, opening the container daily to stir the contents for aeration.

3. After 2 to 3 weeks, strain the contents through cheesecloth or a nut milk bag into sterilized bottles and seal. The vinegar is ready to use now, or it can be fermented for another week or so, until you reach your desired taste. Store the final product in the fridge for up to 6 weeks (if you leave it at room temperature, it will continue fermenting).

CONFIT MUSHROOMS

This recipe is a great way to keep mushrooms plump, firm, and full of flavor while having them in your fridge so you can pull them out whenever you need them. I use them on pizza, but they're great tossed in pasta, in a salad, in an omelet, or just eaten on their own.

1½ lb mushrooms (of your choice)

2 tbsp minced shallots

1 tbsp fresh thyme leaves

2 cups neutral olive oil or grapeseed oil

Salt, to taste

MAKES: 2 CUPS   PREP: 5 MIN   COOK: 40 MIN

1. Clean the mushrooms by wiping them with a damp paper towel. If the stems are edible, simply trim the ends; otherwise, separate the caps from the stems and reserve the stems to make a mushroom broth.

2. In a saucepan, combine the minced shallots, thyme leaves, cleaned mushrooms, and oil. Heat gently for about 40 minutes; you do not want the oil to bubble or the shallots to burn.

3. Remove from heat and cool completely. Season with salt to taste and transfer to a cool, sterilized jar. Store in the fridge for up to 2 weeks.

Porridges + Soups

BLUEBERRY AND BARLEY PORRIDGE, PAGE 32

PORRIDGE

In Jamaica, porridge is *the* way to start your day. It fills you up for a long time, and acts as a blank canvas that can take on different flavors. It feels like there are as many ways to make porridge as there are people in Jamaica! Whenever I return there, I see new varieties of pre-packaged porridge in the markets for people to make at home. It's harder to find such a wide selection outside the island, so I've included some of my favorite porridge recipes for you here.

You'll see that some of my porridges are sweet, and others are savory. That's because there are no rules with porridge; it just needs to taste good. It can be made with all kinds of nuts and grains, but to me, the most traditional type of porridge is cornmeal. I spent a lot of time learning how to get cornmeal porridge just right—it's easy to add too much or too little cornmeal. I developed a technique to slowly fold the cornmeal into the boiling water, so the porridge is the perfect texture every time.

Once you're comfortable with all my flavor recommendations, try playing around a little bit to make your porridge the way you like. And when you're in Jamaica, look for the street vendors rolling around selling porridge—my favorite is peanut porridge. If you get lucky, you'll find it served with flair: I remember seeing one guy pour the porridge out of a pot over his head into a cup he held by his waist. That was some next-level porridge skills.

SPICED CORNMEAL PORRIDGE

1 cup fine cornmeal

1 cup full-fat coconut milk

1 cup pineapple juice

1 tsp salt

1 tsp ground allspice

1 tsp ground nutmeg

1 cinnamon stick

1 cup condensed milk

1 tsp vanilla extract

Fresh pineapple chunks, for serving

Ground cinnamon, for serving

I grew up eating a lot of cornmeal porridge. My mom was the librarian at the school I went to in Jamaica, and she would leave for work before I left for school. Cornmeal porridge was one of the first things she taught me to make so I could prepare breakfast on my own. As I got older, I experimented more with it and started to incorporate coconut, pineapple, and evaporated milk to make it more flavorful and fun. This reminds me of my mom, and I know it would make her so proud that it made its way to these pages.

SERVES: 4   PREP: 2 MIN   COOK: 10 MIN

1. In a medium saucepan, combine the cornmeal, coconut milk, pineapple juice, salt, allspice, nutmeg and cinnamon stick.

2. Heat over medium heat, stirring with a whisk to avoid clumping. Cook the cornmeal until it thickens and has a porridge consistency, around 10 minutes. Add the condensed milk and vanilla, cook for 30 seconds more, then remove from heat.

3. Portion the porridge into bowls and top with pineapple and a sprinkle of ground cinnamon.

BLUEBERRY & BARLEY PORRIDGE

⅓ cup pearled barley

¼ cup oatmeal

1 cup full-fat coconut milk

1 tsp vanilla extract

1 tbsp honey

2 tbsp fresh blueberries (use them fresh or try macerating with a little sugar and fruit juice first)

1 tbsp chopped almonds

1 tbsp coconut flakes

Photo on page 30

This recipe was created by mistake. I was playing around with barley, experimenting with using it like a risotto, and then I tried it in porridge with Ontario blueberries. As soon as I ate it, it reminded me of something I used to have as a kid in Jamaica from a company called Lasco, packets of a soy powder you mixed with water or milk. For my mother, it was an inexpensive way of filling me up. This recipe reminds me of how far I've come.

SERVES: 2   PREP: 10 MIN   COOK: 15 MIN

1. In a spice or coffee grinder, grind the barley and oats until slightly coarse.

2. In a saucepan, dissolve the ground barley and oats in 2 cups water and mix well. Gently heat over medium heat, add the coconut milk, and cook, stirring occasionally, until the porridge has thickened and is smooth and free of clumps, about 10 minutes. Stir in the vanilla and honey, and remove from heat.

3. Portion the porridge into bowls, sprinkle the blueberries, chopped almonds and coconut flakes on top, and serve immediately.

CHOCOLATE RICE PORRIDGE

My girlfriend, Regina, is Filipino, and I have really gotten into her culture and cuisine. They have a dessert called champorado, which is a sweet chocolate rice pudding. I didn't really like it until, one day, a Filipino chef buddy of ours served it warm at his restaurant (he has a really progressive way of making Filipino food), and it was so much better than the cold version. I decided to make it with my Afro-Caribbean twist by adding coconut milk. Now it's a dessert staple in our home, with a little bit of Regina and a little bit of me.

SERVES: 6   PREP: 2 MIN   COOK: 20 MIN

1. In a saucepan, combine the glutinous rice and coconut milk with 1 cup water. Bring to a boil for 10 minutes, stirring occasionally to keep the rice from sticking to the bottom of the pot.

2. Stir in the cocoa powder and salt. Reduce the heat to low, cover, and continue cooking, stirring occasionally, until the rice is tender, about 10 minutes.

3. Remove from heat, add the condensed milk, and stir to combine. Serve hot, topped with your favorite toppings.

1 cup glutinous rice

2 cups full-fat coconut milk

½ cup cocoa powder

1 tsp salt

1½ cups condensed milk

OPTIONAL TOPPINGS

Banana, sliced

Chocolate chips

Fresh blueberries

Unsweetened, shredded coconut

CINNAMON APPLE OVERNIGHT OATS

This was inspired by me not having enough time to make breakfast . . . and having apple pie filling in my fridge. It's literally apple pie meets oatmeal. And it's totally acceptable to eat for breakfast!

SERVES: 2   PREP: 5 MIN + REFRIGERATION   COOK: 5 MIN

½ tbsp unsalted butter

1 cup peeled and medium-diced apples

½ cup brown sugar

1 tsp ground cinnamon

1 tsp ground nutmeg

¼ cup full-fat coconut milk

¼ cup raisins

1 cup rolled oats

TOPPINGS (OPTIONAL)

Apple slices, dusted with cinnamon

Peanut butter

Honey

1. In a medium saucepan over medium-high heat, melt the butter. Add the apples, brown sugar, cinnamon, and nutmeg and cook for 2 to 3 minutes, until the apples are softened.

2. Deglaze your pot with 2 cups water, then add the coconut milk and raisins. Turn the heat up to high and bring to a low boil. Remove from heat and let the liquid cool completely.

3. Transfer the mixture to 2 jars or mugs. Divide the oats between each and mix to combine. Refrigerate overnight.

4. In the morning, serve with apple slices, peanut butter or a drizzle of honey.

COCONUT CARROT PORRIDGE

If you can believe it, the idea for this recipe originally came from a salmon dish I used to make when working as a freelance chef. It's a good reminder that inspiration can come from anywhere. I was working as a temp chef through a staffing agency, and I spent a lot of time in corporate kitchens filling in for executive chefs who needed a vacation but were under-staffed. My assignment for that day was to create a seafood lunch option for the à la carte menu. I rifled through the walk-in fridge but was only able to find some carrots (and even they were on their way out). So I whipped up a carrot sauce and ladled it over well-seasoned salmon with perfectly crispy seared skin. The salmon lunch was an absolute success, but I found myself eating spoonfuls of this sauce on its own, so I decided to further the concept with the addition of condensed milk and raisins and turn it into this porridge.

SERVES: 4   PREP: 10 MIN   COOK: 10 MIN

1. In a medium saucepan, combine the ghee and carrots. Cook over medium heat for 3 minutes, or until the carrots soften.

2. Add the condensed milk, coconut cream, 1 cup water, and the oats and cardamom. Bring to a boil and simmer for 5 to 6 minutes. Remove from heat and let cool for 5 minutes.

3. Transfer to a high-powered blender and blend until smooth.

4. Portion the porridge between bowls and serve with a topping of raisins, a drizzle of coconut cream and a dash of cinnamon.

¼ cup oats

1 tbsp ghee

3 medium carrots, grated

1½ cups condensed milk

¾ cup coconut cream, plus more for serving

1 tsp ground cardamom

1 tbsp raisins, for serving

Ground cinnamon, for serving

COCONUT & CORN SOUP

During the summer of 2019, my long-time friend and fellow chef Bashir Munye reached out to me with the desire to do an event in Toronto that was for us: a safe space where members of the multiethnic Afro-Caribbean community could meet, eat, discuss issues that were of concern to us, and collectively create solutions.

We chose the Black Creek Community Farm as our venue, as the space had so much relevance to our cause: for years, the farm had been doing various programs to ensure food security and sovereignty in the community, so it was only fitting that this be our meeting place. Bashir was extremely clear in his vision for this event: we replaced the chairs and tables with beautiful embroidered cushions and patterned rugs, and we didn't have a head of the table, as we wanted everyone to be equal and grounded, literally and metaphorically. We served a multitude of courses that day, and Bashir bestowed upon me the honor of starting off the dining experience with this coconut and corn soup.

SERVES: 4   PREP: 15 MIN   COOK: 25 MIN

3 tbsp coconut oil

1 onion, chopped

1 tbsp Scotch Bonnet Paste (page 21)

1 tsp ground turmeric

¼ cup canned yellow lentils

4 cups vegetable stock

2 tbsp fresh thyme leaves

1 tbsp Garlic Paste (page 24)

8 cobs fresh corn, husked, silks removed, and kernels cut from cobs

1 potato, medium-diced

1 cup coconut cream, plus more for serving

Unsweetened shredded coconut, toasted

Cayenne or chili powder, for serving

Fresh flat-leaf parsley, chopped, for serving

1. In a large saucepan over high heat, melt the coconut oil. Add the onions, Scotch bonnet paste, and turmeric. Add the lentils and stock and bring to a boil.

2. Add the thyme, garlic paste, and corn cobs (but not kernels). Cover and simmer for 15 to 20 minutes, until the lentils are tender.

3. Add the potatoes and coconut cream. Remove the cobs and discard. Simmer the potatoes until tender, about 15 minutes, then add half of the corn kernels and simmer for 2 minutes.

4. Remove from heat and, using a hand blender, carefully purée the soup mixture until smooth. Add the remaining corn kernels, return to the heat, and simmer for 2 more minutes.

5. Serve immediately, topped with a drizzle of coconut cream, toasted coconut, and fresh parsley.

GREEN PEA & POTATO SOUP

A lot of soups in Afro-Caribbean cuisine use pigeon peas, so I wanted to do something that would look and taste different and be innovative, but still have the same idea behind it. Green peas give this soup a great texture. It's light, colorful, and totally delicious.

SERVES: 4   PREP: 5 MIN   COOK: 25 MIN

1. In a large saucepan over high heat, melt the coconut oil. Add the scallions, onions, ginger, and garlic paste and sauté until the onions are tender, about 5 minutes.

2. Add the sweet potatoes and stock and bring to a boil. Cover and simmer for 10 to 15 minutes, until the sweet potatoes are tender.

3. Stir in the spinach and coconut cream, then remove from heat. Using a hand blender, purée the soup mixture until smooth.

4. Return to the stove over low heat, stir in the green peas, and simmer for 2 minutes. Serve immediately topped with cilantro and chia seeds (or the seeds of your choice) for some crunch.

1 tbsp coconut oil

2 cups chopped scallions

¼ cup chopped white onion

1 tbsp minced fresh ginger

¼ cup Garlic Paste (page 24)

2 cups cubed sweet potatoes

4 cups vegetable stock

1 cup spinach

½ cup coconut cream

3 cups frozen green peas

Fresh cilantro, for serving (optional)

Chia seeds, for serving (optional)

ROASTED TOMATO & WHITE BEAN SOUP

When I don't feel like eating Caribbean cuisine, I like to make this soup—especially in the winter, when I can't get certain ingredients for other favorite recipes. It's a go-to recipe that always satisfies.

SERVES: 4   PREP: 5 MIN   COOK: 35 MIN

SOUP

6 plum tomatoes

¼ cup plus 2 tbsp extra virgin olive oil

½ cup chopped fresh cilantro

½ cup chopped fresh thyme

½ cup chopped fresh basil

1 white onion, medium-diced

1 tbsp Garlic Paste (page 24)

1 tbsp tomato paste

4 cups vegetable stock

2 cups canned white beans, drained

COCONUT CRÈME FRAÎCHE (OPTIONAL)

1 cup coconut cream

Chopped fresh cilantro, for serving

1. Preheat the oven to 425°F.

2. In a mixing bowl, combine the tomatoes, ¼ cup olive oil, and chopped herbs and mix well.

3. Place the tomatoes on a baking sheet and roast until they have collapsed and begin to turn golden around the edges, 20 to 25 minutes.

4. When the tomatoes are almost done roasting, heat 2 tbsp olive oil in a large pot. Add the onions, garlic paste, and tomato paste and cook until the onions are softened and the garlic is fragrant, about 8 minutes.

5. Deglaze the pot with vegetable stock and bring to a boil. Remove from heat and add the roasted tomatoes.

6. Using a hand blender, purée the mixture until smooth. Stir in the beans, return to the heat, and bring to a simmer.

7. If using, make the coconut crème fraîche: In a small mixing bowl, whisk the coconut cream until thickened and emulsified.

8. Serve the soup immediately, topped with coconut crème fraîche if desired, or a sprinkling of cilantro.

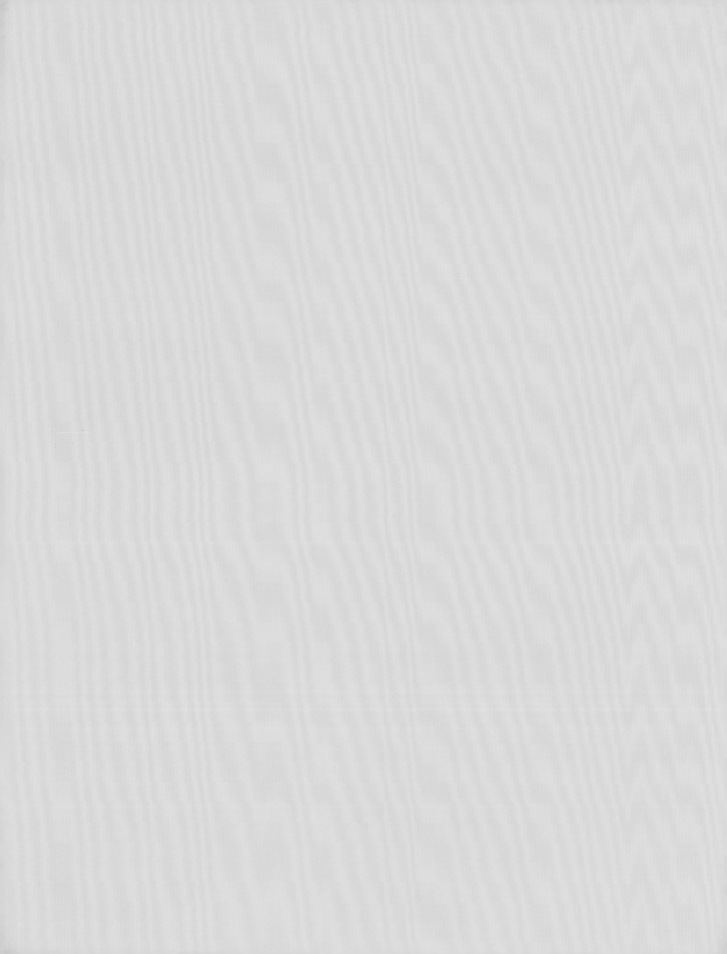

Appetizers

PLANTAIN BREAD

Being an avid consumer of plantains, I often end up buying way too many. As a result, some inevitably become overly ripe and mushy on the inside, so I use them for porridges and my famous beignets (page 215). One day I decided to treat them like bananas and baked a loaf instead.

SERVES: 6   PREP: 20 MIN   COOK: 1½ HR

1. Preheat the oven to 350°F. Grease and flour a 5 × 9-inch loaf pan.

2. In a large mixing bowl, use the back of a fork to mash four of the overripe plantains.

3. In a separate bowl, use a whisk to cream together the butter, sugar, vanilla, and umami paste. Add the coconut milk and then the eggs, one at a time, and keep whisking until incorporated.

4. Use a spatula to fold in the mashed plantains, then slowly add the flour, baking soda, and baking powder. Continue mixing until all the ingredients have been incorporated properly.

5. Using your spatula, pour the batter into the prepared loaf pan.

6. Slice the remaining plantain lengthwise and arrange the halves on top of the batter, side by side, with the cut side facing up.

7. Bake for 1½ hours, or until a toothpick inserted in the center comes out clean.

8. Let cool for at least 30 minutes before removing from the loaf pan.

5 overripe plantains (black skin)
1 cup unsalted butter, softened
1 cup brown sugar
1 tsp vanilla extract
⅓ cup Umami Paste (page 25)
½ cup full-fat coconut milk
2 large eggs
1½ cups all-purpose flour
1 tsp baking soda
1 tsp baking powder

TRINIDADIAN DOUBLES

A doubles is basically two fried turmeric flatbreads, known as bara (made from a yeasty dough similar to donuts), with channa, a spicy chickpea mixture, in the middle. This is a Trinidadian late-night party food that you eat after you come back from the bars or clubs, and I am totally obsessed with them—they're pure magic in your mouth. Trust me: you have to have a doubles before you die.

SERVES: 4   PREP TIME: 35 MIN + RISING   COOK: 45 MIN

BARA

1¼ cups warm (100°F) water

1½ tbsp granulated sugar

2 tsp active dry yeast

3 cups all-purpose flour

2 tsp salt

1 tsp ground cumin or curry powder

1 tsp ground turmeric

Vegetable oil, for greasing

2 cups canola oil, for frying

CHANNA

2 tbsp coconut oil

1 medium onion, chopped

1 tbsp Garlic Paste (page 24)

3 cups canned chickpeas, rinsed and drained

1 tsp puréed fresh ginger

2 cups vegetable stock

3 tbsp curry powder

2 tsp ground cumin

1 tsp smoked paprika

1 tbsp vegetable bouillon powder

1 tsp lemon juice

1 tsp salt

TAMARIND SAUCE

¾ cup tamarind pulp

¼ cup honey or maple syrup

1 tbsp Scotch Bonnet Paste (page 21)

1. Make the bara dough: In a measuring cup, combine the warm water, sugar, and yeast and use a fork to stir. Let stand until foamy, about 5 minutes.

2. In a medium bowl, stir together the flour, salt, cumin or curry powder, and turmeric. Gradually add the yeast mixture to the flour mixture, beating with a fork until completely incorporated, about 2 minutes. Continue beating with a wooden spoon until the dough is smooth and glossy but still sticky, about 5 minutes.

3. Lightly grease a large bowl with oil. Transfer the dough to the bowl and cover tightly with plastic wrap. Let stand at warm room temperature (72°F) until doubled in size, about 1 to 1½ hours.

4. Make the channa: In a cast-iron skillet over medium heat, melt the coconut oil. Add the onions and garlic paste and cook, stirring occasionally, until the onions are softened, about 5 minutes. Stir in the chickpeas, ginger, stock, curry powder, cumin, paprika, bouillon powder and 3 cups water. Cook, stirring occasionally, until liquid is reduced to a syrupy consistency, 25 to 30 minutes. Stir in the lemon juice and salt. Reduce the heat to low and simmer until serving.

5. Make the tamarind sauce: In a saucepan, combine the tamarind pulp, honey or maple syrup, Scotch bonnet paste, and ½ cup water and bring to a boil. Mix well, remove from heat, and set aside.

6. Prepare the bara dough: Turn the bara dough out onto a lightly floured work surface and divide it evenly into 16 pieces (photos 1 + 2). Shape each dough piece into a ball. Cover the balls with a clean towel to prevent the dough from drying out.

7. Lightly dust one dough ball with flour and use a rolling pin to roll it out into a 5-inch round (about ⅛ inch thick). Repeat with remaining dough balls (photo 3).

CONTINUED

Thinly sliced or shaved
   cucumbers (optional)
Scotch Bonnet Paste (page 21)
   (optional)

8. Fry the bara: Pour the canola oil into a deep pan and heat over medium heat to 360°F. Carefully place one or two dough rounds in the hot oil and fry until slightly puffed and the edges look dry, 10 to 15 seconds. Flip and fry on the other side until the bara is just cooked through, about 20 seconds (photo 4). Transfer to a baking sheet lined with paper towels to soak up any excess oil. Repeat with all remaining dough balls.

9. To assemble, place a bara on a plate, then spoon ½ cup of the channa on top. Drizzle with a liberal amount of tamarind sauce, about 1 to 2 tbsp. If you like, garnish with thinly sliced or shaved cucumbers and, if you want an extra kick, a dollop of the Scotch bonnet paste (in Trini they refer to this style as "slight peppah"). Traditionally, you would add another bara on top, but I like to fold them over like a taco.

SIKIL P'AK

I went to Mexico City for my leap-year birthday in 2019, and my girlfriend and I ate at the restaurant Pujol, where they served a pumpkin-seed salsa, sikil p'ak, that I fell hard for. When we made our way to Oaxaca, the chef at the place we were staying made it all the time. I literally ate it every day; I couldn't get enough of it (and quite honestly, I think I overdid it). When I went back to Toronto, I realized that no one there made it, so I developed my own version, incorporating some Scotch bonnet oil. In my opinion, it should be just as popular as salsa and guacamole. Everyone should know about this!

MAKES: 2 CUPS   **PREP: 5 MIN**   **COOK: 10 MIN**

1. Heat your skillet over medium-high heat. Add the pumpkin seeds and cook, swirling the pan often, until lightly toasted, about 3 minutes.

2. Transfer to a food processor and process until smooth, about 45 seconds, then scrape into a bowl and set aside.

3. Return the skillet to high heat and add the Scotch bonnet oil, onions, and tomatoes, turning as needed. Once the tomatoes are charred and tender, about 7 minutes, transfer to the food processor and pulse until they are chunky.

4. Return the pumpkin seeds to the food processor, add the cilantro, chives, and garlic paste, and pulse until smooth. Season to taste and transfer to a cool, sterilized jar. Store in the fridge for up to 2 weeks.

1½ cups unshelled pumpkin seeds

1 tbsp Scotch Bonnet Oil (page 20)

½ cup chopped onion

2 plum tomatoes

3 tbsp chopped fresh cilantro

3 tbsp chopped fresh chives

1 tbsp Garlic Paste (page 24)

Salt, to taste

MANGO CHOW

Here's another Trinidadian classic. I like to think of this recipe as the Afro-Caribbean community's version of the Mexican mangonada or chamango—a chilled tropical fruit snack. Its savory, sweet, spicy, and delicious.

SERVES: 4   PREP: 15 MIN   COOK: N/A

4 semi-ripe mangoes (green-skinned)

1 tbsp Garlic Paste (page 24)

½ tsp Garum Fish Sauce (page 23)

1 tsp Scotch Bonnet Paste (page 21)

2 tbsp chopped shado beni (see introduction on page 26) or fresh cilantro

1. Peel your mangoes and dice the mango pulp into small pieces. Place in a large bowl with all the other ingredients and toss together.

2. Chill in the fridge for at least 30 minutes to allow the ingredients to marinate.

3. Serve chilled as a snack or on the side as a salad.

ZUCCHINI CRUDO

I hosted a lot of dinner parties while doing recipe development in Turks and Caicos, and one of the crowd-pleasers was this crudo. The original concept was with a Turks specialty, conch (sea snail), but since I like a good challenge, I reimagined this dish with a new key ingredient: zucchini.

SERVES: 4   PREP: 10 MIN   COOK: N/A

1. In a large stainless-steel bowl, combine the Scotch bonnet paste, garlic paste, pineapple vinegar, and herb oil and whisk until fully emulsified.

2. Cut the ends off the zucchinis to make them each about 5 inches long. Use a mandoline to shave thin slices from each zucchini.

3. Place the sliced zucchinis in the bowl with the Scotch bonnet marinade and mix well. Chill in the fridge for 10 minutes.

4. Arrange the zucchini slices on a serving plate, overlapping and alternating between yellow and green slices. Season with salt and pepper.

5. Top with the navel orange segments and a sprinkle of capers. Finish by drizzling a tablespoon of the marinade over the crudo and a sprinkle of red pepper flakes, if desired.

1 tbsp Scotch Bonnet Paste (page 21)

1 tbsp Garlic Paste (page 24)

¼ cup Pineapple Vinegar (page 27)

¼ cup Herb Oil (page 26)

1 medium yellow zucchini

1 medium green zucchini

Salt and freshly ground black pepper, to taste

1 navel orange, segmented

Handful of capers (optional), for serving

Red pepper flakes, for serving

LOBSTER CRUDO

I spent a lot of time in Turks and Caicos during the pandemic, and this recipe came from me and some other chefs freestyling with ingredients down at the beach. It's fresh, light, summery, and totally delicious.

SERVES: 4   PREP: 10 MIN + MARINATING   COOK: N/A

8 oz lobster tail

¼ cup fresh orange juice

2 tbsp fresh lemon juice

2 tbsp fresh lime juice

1 tbsp extra virgin olive oil

Chopped scallions, for serving

Salt and freshly ground black pepper

JERK APPLE SALSA

½ McIntosh or other tart apple, diced

1 shallot, diced

1 tbsp Jerk Marinade (page 19)

1. Remove the lobster meat from the shell and cut it in half lengthwise, then into ½-inch pieces.

2. In a nonreactive stainless-steel bowl, combine the juices of the three citrus fruits. Add the chopped lobster and chill in the fridge to for at least 1 hour, and up to 3 or 4 hours (this process "cooks" the lobster, but any longer and the lobster starts to get rubbery in texture).

3. Meanwhile, make the jerk apple salsa: In a small bowl, combine the apples, shallots, and jerk marinade and mix well. Start by adding the jerk marinade a little at a time—the more you add, the hotter the sauce will become, and the darker in color.

4. Remove the bowl of lobster from the fridge and pour the citrus dressing onto a large rimmed plate. Arrange the lobster over the plate.

5. Spoon jerk apple salsa on top. Garnish with olive oil, chopped scallions and season lightly with salt and pepper.

SCALLOP CEVICHE

During the winter of 2016, I was burnt out from working 16-hour days for 2 consecutive years trying to build a chicken and waffle empire. With the encouragement of my then-business partner, I took 10 days off for vacation and visited Cuba. On my first night in town, I visited a local restaurant for dinner, and the server brought over a small complimentary bowl of snapper ceviche before the actual meal. Up until that point, I didn't know much about consuming "uncooked" seafood—I had worked as an executive chef of a seafood restaurant, but all our proteins were cooked! I like to consider myself a very adventurous eater—my mantra for life is "try anything twice"—so I dove in. And loved it! Since that night, I don't think I've gone longer than 3 consecutive days without eating some sort of sashimi, crudo, tartare, or ceviche. This is my all-time favorite ceviche recipe, and it's my go-to because it's simple, healthy, and quick.

SERVES: 4   PREP: 10 MIN + MARINATING   COOK: N/A

1. In a nonreactive stainless-steel bowl, whisk together the coconut water, pineapple vinegar, lemon juice, sugar, and garlic paste.

2. Stir in the Scotch bonnet paste, tomatoes, onions, and scallops and mix very well. Chill in the fridge for 10 minutes (and not more than 30 minutes) until the scallops turn opaque.

3. Season with salt and pepper to taste (adding more sugar will reduce the tartness). Garnish with avocado, if desired, and serve immediately.

¼ cup coconut water

2 Tbsp Pineapple Vinegar (page 27)

Juice of 1 lemon

1 tbsp brown sugar

1 tbsp Garlic Paste (page 24)

1 tsp Scotch Bonnet Paste (page 21)

2 plum tomatoes, medium-diced

1 cup small-diced white onions

1 lb bay scallops, quartered

Salt and freshly ground black pepper, to taste

1 firm, ripe avocado, peeled, pitted, and diced (optional)

ACKEE & SALTFISH FRITTERS

Ackee and saltfish is as Jamaican as apple pie is American, so much so that it's the official national dish of the island. I developed this fritter recipe to celebrate Jamaica's national dish, do my part to preserve an ancestral food, and introduce other eaters to an exciting ingredient they might not have heard of before.

SERVES: 6, MAKES: 24 FRITTERS   **PREP: 15 MIN + SOAKING**   **COOK: 20 MIN**

FRITTERS

16 oz (2 to 3 fillets) salted cod (to make about 2 cups soaked and shredded)

¾ cup all-purpose flour

1 tsp baking powder

1¼ tsp fresh thyme leaves

2 scallions, chopped

½ cup pumpkin purée

1 tbsp Scotch Bonnet Paste (page 21)

1 egg

2 cups canned ackee, mashed to a pulp

2 cups vegetable oil, for frying

MANGO MAYONNAISE

¼ cup puréed mango

Zest of 1 lime

1 tbsp lime juice

1 egg yolk

½ tsp salt

1 cup vegetable oil

1. Soak the salted cod in water for a couple of hours to remove excess salt (alternatively, you can boil it, drain, and then bring it to a boil again).

2. Make the mango mayonnaise: In a food processor or blender, combine the mango purée, lime zest and juice, egg yolk, and salt. Cover and mix for a few seconds. Turn to the lowest speed and, with the machine running, add the oil in a thin, steady stream through the opening in the lid. The mayonnaise will emulsify quickly, in less than a minute. If necessary, turn off the processor or blender and scrape the sides of the bowl so the blades can reach the ingredients. Store in an airtight container in the fridge for up to 2 weeks.

3. When the cod is ready, use a fork to shred it into a large nonreactive stainless-steel bowl. Add the flour, baking powder, thyme, and scallions and mix well. Add the pumpkin purée, Scotch bonnet paste, egg, and ⅓ cup water and continue mixing until the dough is just thicker than a pancake batter (add a little more water as needed).

4. Once the dough has reached the right consistency, slowly fold in the ackee, trying not to mush it too much.

5. In a large nonstick frying pan over medium-high heat, heat the oil to 350°F.

6. Working in batches, use an ice cream scoop to drop 6 scoops of the mixture into the oil. Fry until golden brown and the fritters begin to float. Transfer the fritters to a tray lined with paper towel or a wire rack, to drain off excess oil. Repeat in batches of 6, for a total of 24 fritters.

7. Let cool for 5 minutes, then serve with mango mayonnaise!

CASSAVA & COD LATKES

I developed this recipe when I was working on a food TV show, behind the scenes. I wanted to take a dish that lots of people are familiar with and give it my Caribbean twist. In Jamaica, we eat a lot of salted cod and cassava, so why not try a Jamaican-style latke?

MAKES: 12 (4-INCH) LATKES   **PREP: 15 MIN + SOAKING**   **COOK: 30 MIN**

1. Soak the cod in water for a couple of hours to remove excess salt (alternatively, you can boil the cod, drain it, and then bring it to a boil again). When the cod is ready, use a fork to shred it into a large non-reactive stainless-steel bowl.

2. In a separate large bowl, combine the flour, salt, sugar, and ¾ cup water and mix well. Add the eggs and whisk until emulsified and free of lumps.

3. Fold in the chopped cabbage, shredded cod, and dried shrimp and continue to mix until fully incorporated. Let this batter rest while preparing the cassava.

4. Using a box grater, grate the cassava roots. Wrap in cheesecloth and squeeze to remove excess liquid. Transfer the grated cassava to the bowl with the batter and fold in until fully incorporated.

5. Heat the oil a large skillet or cast-iron pan over medium-low heat until it reaches 300°F.

6. Working in batches, use a ladle to add about four scoops (about ½ cup each) of cassava batter to the pan; be careful not to crowd the pan.

7. When the edge of the latkes become firm and cooked, 4 to 5 minutes per side, use a spatula to flip them. Adjust the heat if necessary so they don't burn. Transfer the latkes to a wire rack placed on top of a baking sheet to drain any excess oil for 2 minutes. Repeat in batches of 4, for a total of 12 latkes.

8. Season with salt and serve immediately with apple sauce or sour cream or the dip of your choice, and sprinkled with chopped scallions.

8 oz (1 to 2 fillets) salted cod (to make about 1 cup soaked and shredded)

1¼ cups all-purpose flour

1 tsp salt

¼ tsp granulated sugar

4 medium eggs, room temperature

¾ cup chopped green cabbage

4 tbsp dried shrimp

1 lb cassava, peeled (about 3 to 4 roots)

¼ cup neutral oil (like canola or grapeseed)

Apple sauce or sour cream, for serving

Chopped scallions, for serving

CARIBBEAN CRAB DIP

When I was on *Top Chef Canada*, I would host viewing parties with family and friends when each episode aired. I would make the dish I did on the show for them to enjoy as we watched. Since I didn't make it to the end, for the semifinal I chose to make this crab dip for everyone instead. Serve it on fries and add gravy (poutine-style), or put it in a wrap, or add it to grilled cheese . . . whatever makes you happy.

SERVES: 4   PREP: 5 MIN   COOK: 5 MIN

2 cups cream cheese

2 cups fresh or canned lump crab meat

2 cups shredded cheddar

1 cup mayonnaise

2 scallions, chopped

1 clove garlic, minced

1 tbsp lemon juice

1 tsp Jerk Marinade (page 19)

Crostini or tortilla chips, for serving

1. In a bowl, combine the cream cheese, the crab meat, half of the cheddar, and the mayonnaise, scallions, garlic, lemon juice, and jerk marinade. Mix well.

2. Transfer to an 8 oz ramekin or a greased cast-iron skillet, and top with the remaining cheddar. Broil in the oven on high for 5 minutes. Serve with crostini or tortilla chips.

JERK-MARINATED PORK ANTICUCHOS

I like to consider myself a student of life. I'm a firm believer that the moment you stop learning, you've stopped living. I have an unspoken rule that I won't refer to any of my fellow industry colleagues as "chef" until they have taught me something. When I first met my sous-chef, Alex Fields, he did not know much about Afro-Caribbean cuisine. He worked at a very swanky and upscale Peruvian restaurant in Toronto. Our first while together, we spent most of our time explaining different recipes and learning techniques from our respective styles of cooking. I decided to pay him a surprise visit during his last week of employment at that restaurant before he came to work for me full time. He treated me to an amazing five-course meal that surpassed my already high expectations, and the highlight of the night was the anticuchos. Anticuchos are a popular street food in Peru, where beef hearts are marinated in vinegar, cumin, aji pepper, and garlic, and then grilled on a skewer. We've since combined our collective knowledge of Peruvian and Afro-Caribbean cuisines to develop an anticuchos recipe that we are both extremely proud of. Needless to say, he goes by "chef" to me now.

SERVES: 4   PREP: 10 MIN   COOK: 20 MIN

1. Prepare the pork loin: In a large bowl, combine the jerk marinade, soy sauce, vegetable oil, and cumin and whisk to form a paste. Add the cubed pork to the bowl, mix well, and allow to marinate for 10 minutes.

2. Heat your indoor or outdoor grill to medium-high heat, about 450°F.

3. Thread the cubes of pork evenly onto metal skewers. Place the skewers on the grill and brush on the remaining marinade. Grill until the marinade has caramelized, about 10 to 15 minutes.

4. Make the mango chutney: In a saucepan, combine the mangoes, onions, pineapple vinegar, garum fish sauce, and honey and bring to a boil. Remove from heat, add the bell peppers and chives, and mix well.

5. Arrange the skewers on a plate, then spoon a good amount of chutney over each skewer. Serve with fresh lime wedges and enjoy!

NOTE: *As a quick, fresh alternative to the Mango Chutney, you can top your skewers with a mix of finely chopped fresh mango, red onion and fresh herbs (as pictured opposite).*

PORK LOIN
1 cup Jerk Marinade (page 19)

½ cup soy sauce

½ cup vegetable oil

1 tbsp ground cumin

1½ lb pork loin, cut into 1-inch cubes

MANGO CHUTNEY
1 ripe mango, diced

½ red onion, diced

⅓ cup Pineapple Vinegar (page 27)

1 tbsp Garum Fish Sauce (page 23)

1 tbsp honey

1 red bell pepper, diced

1 tbsp chopped fresh chives

Lime wedges (optional), for serving

CURRY CHICKEN SPRING ROLLS

I was once hired as a private chef for a well-known comedian, and he was totally obsessed with spring rolls. He wanted me to make him a different spring roll every day. The first few days were fine, but by day four, I was trying to figure out how to make it more interesting. I had leftover curry chicken from the night before, so I decided to use it in the spring roll. Thankfully, he loved it. Even I have to admit, these are pretty damn good.

SERVES: 4, MAKES: 16 SPRING ROLLS   **PREP: 15 MIN**   **COOK: 4 HR**

1. Prepare the spring roll filling: In your slow cooker, combine the curry paste, coconut milk, chicken stock, thyme, ginger, Scotch bonnet paste, onions, and scallions and mix well.

2. Add the chicken breasts and mix well to make sure the chicken is fully immersed in the cooking liquid. Cover and cook on low heat for 3½ hours.

3. Remove the chicken breasts from the slow cooker. Using two forks, pull the chicken apart until completely shredded.

4. Return the chicken to the slow cooker and mix well. Transfer everything to a mixing bowl and set aside.

5. Make the coconut aioli: In a small mixing bowl, combine the coconut cream, garlic paste, lime juice, and salt and whisk until emulsified. Set aside.

6. Assemble and fry the spring rolls: Place the spring roll wrappers on a work surface. Place 2 tbsp of the chicken filling in the center of each. Tuck the ends in, then roll them up and seal the edges with the beaten egg (photos 1 + 2 below).

7. In a wok or heavy skillet, heat the vegetable oil to 350°F. When the oil is hot, add the spring rolls, in batches of four at a time, and deep-fry for 3 minutes, or until golden brown.

8. Transfer to a baking sheet lined with paper towels to soak up any excess oil. Repeat with all remaining spring rolls. Serve hot with the coconut aioli dipping sauce.

SPRING ROLLS

½ cup Curry Paste (page 21)
2 cups full-fat coconut milk
1 cup chicken stock
1¼ tsp fresh thyme leaves
1 tsp ground ginger
1 tbsp Scotch Bonnet Paste (page 21)
½ cup diced onion
2 scallions, chopped
2 lb boneless, skinless chicken breasts
16 store-bought spring roll wrappers
1 egg, beaten
2 cups vegetable oil, for frying

COCONUT AIOLI

1 cup coconut cream
1 tbsp Garlic Paste (page 24)
1 tbsp lime juice
½ tsp salt

OXTAIL NACHOS

The night the finale of my season of *Top Chef Canada* aired, I served these nachos at the viewing party I hosted for my family and friends. It's the perfect Caribbean twist on the perfect party food.

SERVES: 4   PREP: 15 MIN   COOK: 25 MIN

TORTILLA CHIPS
12 corn tortillas
1 cup vegetable oil
Salt

CHEESE SAUCE
2 tbsp unsalted butter
2 tbsp all-purpose flour
1 cup full-fat coconut milk
1½ cups shredded medium
   cheddar cheese
2 tbsp Garlic Paste (page 24)

2 cups Oxtail Ragu (page 201)

TOPPINGS (OPTIONAL)
3 Pickled Scotch Bonnets
   (page 20), sliced
¼ cup chopped scallions
1 cup diced red onions
1 cup medium-diced pineapple
1 cup medium-diced tomatoes
Lime wedges, for serving

1. Make the tortilla chips: Cut each tortilla into six triangle-shaped wedges. Line a plate with paper towel, and have some extra paper towel handy in case you need it.

2. In a frying pan, heat the vegetable oil to 350°F. Working in batches, place a single layer of tortilla triangles into the hot oil (about six to eight pieces should fit at a time). Fry for about 2 minutes, until the triangles just begin to color and become firm and no longer pliable. Transfer the chips to the prepared plate and season with salt. Continue until all the tortilla triangles have been fried.

3. Make the cheese sauce: In a small saucepan over medium heat, whisk the butter and flour together until they become bubbly and foamy.

4. Whisk the coconut milk into the flour and butter mixture. Turn the heat up slightly and allow the milk to come to a simmer while whisking. When it reaches a simmer, the mixture will thicken. Once it's thick enough to coat a spoon, turn off the heat. Stir in the cheddar, one handful at a time, until melted into the sauce. Once all the cheese is melted into the sauce, whisk in the garlic paste.

5. Finish the nachos: Spread half of the tortilla chips out on a dinner plate in a single layer. Add 1 cup cheese sauce, then 1 cup oxtail ragu, then half of each of your toppings. Add the second layer of tortilla chips, then the remainder of the cheese sauce and oxtail ragu. Finish with the second half of your toppings, and serve with lime wedges.

NOTE: *Feel free to take a shortcut with this recipe and use store-bought tortilla chips instead of making your own (as shown opposite). Add the toppings you like for your nachos—just don't skip the Oxtail Ragu or cheese sauce!*

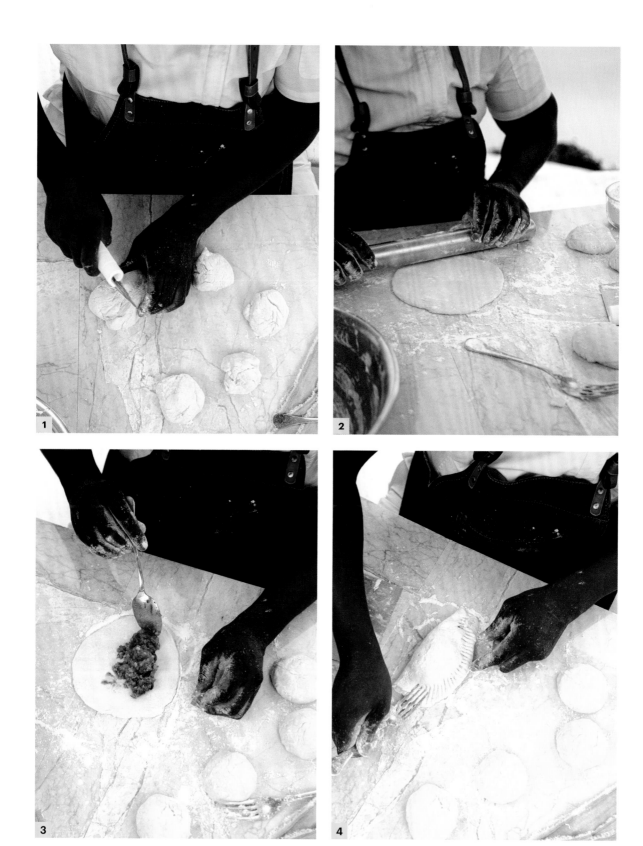

BULLY BEEF EMPANADAS

Canned foods are staple items in many Caribbean households. I grew up eating canned sardines, jack mackerel, Vienna sausages, lunch meat, and corned beef. This recipe is a recreation of one of my childhood favorites, "bully beef," which is canned corned beef cooked down with aromatics, fresh herbs, and spices, then served with traditional Jamaican johnny-cakes (which are kind of like Southern-style biscuits). Here I turn the corned beef filling into delicious empanadas instead, served with a ginger aioli on the side.

SERVES: 6   PREP: 20 MIN   COOK: 35 MIN

1. Make the dough: In a mixing bowl, combine the Grace Festival mix with the coconut milk and mix well. Knead lightly with your hands. Cover the mixing bowl with a damp cloth and leave the dough to sit for about 15 minutes.

2. On a floured surface, separate the dough into two equal halves. Cut those halves into equal thirds so you have six balls of dough (photo 1). Set aside while you make the filling.

3. Make the filling: In a large skillet or frying pan, melt the coconut oil over high heat. Add the onions, garlic paste, tomatoes, and thyme and cook, stirring occasionally, until the onions are softened, about 5 minutes. Stir in the corned beef and Scotch bonnet and continue to mix well. Remove from heat and let cool.

4. Make the ginger aioli: In a small mixing bowl, combine the mayonnaise, garlic paste, ginger, and fish sauce. Whisk very well.

5. Make the empanadas: On the floured surface, roll out each dough ball into a 4- to 5-inch round (photo 2). Add ¼ cup of meat filling to the center of each and fold the dough over in half to enclose the filling (photo 3). Use a fork to press and seal the edges closed (photo 4). You can refrigerate the uncooked empanadas for up to 3 hours.

6. When ready to fry, pour the canola oil into a deep pan and heat over medium heat to 360°F. Fry the empanadas until golden brown, about 6 to 7 minutes.

7. Serve immediately with the ginger aioli on the side.

DOUGH
1 (270 g) package Grace Festival (dough mix)
½ cup full-fat coconut milk
2 cups canola oil, for frying

FILLING
2 tbsp coconut oil
1 medium onion, chopped
1 tbsp Garlic Paste (page 24)
1 plum tomato, chopped
1 tbsp chopped fresh thyme
1 (12 oz) can corned beef
1 Scotch bonnet pepper, minced

GINGER AIOLI
2 tbsp mayonnaise
1 tbsp Garlic Paste (page 24)
1 tbsp minced fresh ginger
1 tsp fish sauce

Photo on page 78

JAMAICAN PATTIES

I can't think of a food more Jamaican than patties; I love seeing people going crazy for them in different parts of the world. Like so much good food, their beauty is in their simplicity. There are just two parts: the filling and the crust. The classic filling is ground beef seasoned with a heavy hand, but you will find all types of flavors available. The crust is a flaky pastry dough, with some turmeric in the mix to give it that signature golden color. You might be wondering why I haven't included a patty recipe in this book. Trust me; it's not out of disrespect for the patty! It's the opposite: I don't think I'll ever get one as good as I know they can be—for those, you need to go to the home of the ultimate patty: Mother's.

Mother's is a really popular casual restaurant chain in Jamaica, and they are undeniably the masters. When I was young, I would go there with my mom—who was my school's librarian—after school. As I got older, nothing would make me happier than eating patties from Mother's while hanging out with my buddies after school at the Half Way Tree station (the bus terminal where it was all happening, good and bad). I was at an all-boys school, so we'd get fresh again when school came out—doing our hair, shining our shoes—and catch the bus there. My friends might have been there to meet girls, but it was all about the patties for me: a dozen to share, all kinds of fillings, and some Chubbys to drink.

I've never been able to replicate the taste and the texture of the patties at Mother's. As a chef, it bugs me when I can't make the best version of something. But I won't leave you hanging completely— that's why I included a recipe for Jamaican Tourtières (page 80). They have the same style of filling and pastry as a classic beef patty, but I borrowed the shape from Canadian tourtière to create something that feels like my own.

JAMAICAN TOURTIÈRES

This recipe is inspired by my Jamaican roots and my love of Canada. There's nothing more Canadian than tourtière-style meat pies, but this recipe uses a filling like that of a Jamaican patty. Let's just say it's the best of both worlds.

SERVES: 4   PREP: 15 MIN   COOK: 35 MIN

DOUGH

1½ cups all-purpose flour

1 tsp ground turmeric

¼ tsp salt

¼ cup unsalted butter or vegetable shortening

1 egg, beaten

FILLING

1½ lb ground beef

1 small onion, diced

1 tbsp Garlic Paste (page 24)

1½ tsp salt

1 tsp dried thyme

½ tsp ground cinnamon

½ tsp ground cloves

3 tbsp all-purpose flour

⅓ cup beef stock

1 tbsp Scotch Bonnet Paste (page 21)

1 tbsp store-bought caramelized browning (see Note)

Chopped scallions (optional), for serving

1. Preheat the oven to 425°F.

2. Make the dough: In a large bowl, combine the flour with the turmeric and salt. Cut in the butter or shortening until the mixture is a roughly even crumbly texture. Add 3 tbsp ice water and blend until the dough comes together.

3. Remove the dough from the bowl and shape into a rough disk. Wrap in plastic wrap and chill in the fridge while you prepare the filling.

4. Make the filling: In a skillet over medium-high heat, combine the beef, onions, garlic paste, salt, thyme, cinnamon, and cloves and cook for 5 minutes.

5. Add the flour and stir, then add the beef stock and stir again. Bring to a boil, then reduce the heat and simmer until the meat is cooked through, about 5 minutes. Add the Scotch bonnet paste and caramelized browning and cook for another 2 to 3 minutes.

6. On a lightly floured surface, unwrap the dough, cut into four equal parts, and roll them into balls. Then, using a rolling pin, roll each ball flat into a circle, about 4½ inches in diameter (depending on the size of your ramekins) and ¼ inch thick.

7. Fill four large, 12 to 16 oz ramekins with an equal amount of meat in each. Lay one dough round over the top of each ramekin. Using a fork, press the dough down to meet the rim, then use a paring knife to trim away any excess overhang.

8. Brush the dough with the beaten egg and bake in the oven until the pastry is golden brown, about 15 minutes. Serve hot with a sprinkle of scallions on top.

NOTE: *Caramelized browning is a pantry staple used in Afro-Caribbean cuisine that's available to buy in stores. It's made by reducing caramelized cane sugar with vegetable concentrates, seasonings, and water until it reaches a syrup consistency. It adds both flavor and color to sweet and savory dishes, and can be used in soups, stews, marinades, and sauces.*

Salads

CRISPY OKRA SLAW

I got the inspiration for this dish from my friend chef Bashir Munye. Bashir often cooks with okra and served an iteration of this salad at one of our Black Creek Community Farm dinners (see page 20). A lot of people are afraid of cooking with okra, but this dish is a great introduction. It works as a fresh side to any meat, fish, or chicken dish or can be eaten as a salad on its own.

SERVES: 4   PREP: 10 MIN   COOK: 25 MIN

1. Preheat the oven to 450°F.

2. Trim the okra by cutting away the stem ends and the tips—just the very ends. Then cut the okra in half lengthwise.

3. Place the okra in a large bowl. Add the coconut oil and berbere and stir to coat the okra halves.

4. Place the okra on a baking sheet in a single layer. Roast in the oven for 20 to 25 minutes, shaking or stirring at least twice during the roasting time.

5. Once the okra is golden brown and crispy, remove from the oven and add back to the mixing bowl.

6. Add the tomatoes, parsley, lemon juice, red onions, and a little of the tahini and mix well. Season with salt to taste, and more tahini as desired.

1 lb okra

2 tbsp coconut oil, melted

1 tbsp berbere spice (or smoked paprika)

1 medium tomato, cored, seeded, and julienned

¼ cup chopped fresh flat-leaf parsley

2 tbsp lemon juice

½ cup thinly sliced red onions

About ½ cup tahini

Salt, to taste

CONDENSED MILK SLAW

Back in 2017, when I had my restaurant AF1 Caribbean Canteen, a few customers voiced their concern that they could never enjoy my coleslaw because of egg allergies. Being the people-pleaser that I am, I started working on a non-mayonnaise version. Everyone loved it so much, I switched to the new version entirely.

SERVES: 10   PREP: 20 MIN   COOK: N/A

SLAW

½ head purple cabbage, finely shredded

½ head green cabbage, finely shredded

3 medium carrots, shredded

½ cup sliced white onions

½ cup chopped scallions

DRESSING

¼ cup Pineapple Vinegar (page 27)

1 tsp Garlic Paste (page 24)

1 tbsp Scotch Bonnet Oil (page 20)

1 (14 oz) can sweetened condensed milk

1. Make the slaw: Place all the shredded cabbage in a very large bowl (you should have about 6 to 8 cups). Add the carrots, onions, and scallions and toss to mix.

2. Make the dressing: In a separate bowl, combine the pineapple vinegar, garlic paste, Scotch bonnet oil, and condensed milk and whisk until all the ingredients are incorporated.

3. Pour a third of your dressing over the cabbage mixture and stir well, ensuring all the ingredients are evenly coated. Taste and add more dressing if you like.

4. Eat right away or let the slaw marinate in the fridge for about an hour to let the flavors develop and the cabbage soften. Store leftover dressing in an airtight container in the fridge for up to 7 days, and use to spread on sandwiches or to add to potato salad.

OG POTATO SALAD

My grandmother was a devout Christian, an elder in her church, and very well known for her cooking. Whenever we would attend church gatherings, the congregation would always request her food, specifically her roasted chicken and famous potato salad. Lucky for me (and you!), I was able to memorize all the potato salad ingredients so I could fine-tune and share the recipe.

SERVES: 8   PREP: 15 MIN   COOK: 20 MIN

1. Bring a large pot of water to a boil. Reduce the heat to medium for a lightly rolling boil. Add the salt and stir continuously until the salt is dissolved.

2. Add the potatoes and cook for 20 minutes, or until they are easily pierced with a fork or paring knife. Drain and set aside until just cool enough to handle. Transfer to a large mixing bowl.

3. In a small mixing bowl, combine the mayonnaise, lemon juice, seasoned salt, onion powder, garlic paste, and pepper and whisk everything together.

4. Pour the mayonnaise mixture over the potatoes. Add the celery, onions, and green peas and mix well. Add the egg quarters and continue to mix. Taste and adjust the seasoning as needed. Refrigerate for 10 minutes before serving.

¼ cup salt (for boiling potatoes)

1 lb medium white potatoes, peeled and cut into ½- to ¾-inch cubes

1½ cups mayonnaise

¼ cup lemon juice

1 tbsp seasoned salt (I like Lawry's or Johnny's)

1 tbsp onion powder

½ tbsp Garlic Paste (page 24)

½ tsp freshly ground black pepper

2 large stalks celery, finely chopped

½ cup finely chopped white onions

1½ cups green peas, blanched

6 hard-boiled eggs, peeled and quartered

Salt and freshly ground black pepper, to taste

WATERMELON "POKE"

When you're living on a Caribbean island and a lot of your food comes in on a shipping container twice a week, you get pretty used to improvising when you can't get certain ingredients. This is exactly what happened when I couldn't get tuna for my poke bowls. I replaced the tuna with watermelon and created a pretty awesome, fresh, and healthy dish.

SERVES: 4   PREP: 10 MIN + MARINATING   COOK: 10 MIN

4 cups cubed watermelon (roughly ½-inch cubes)

3 tbsp mushroom soy sauce

2 tbsp Pineapple Vinegar (page 27)

2 tbsp lime juice

1 tbsp Scotch Bonnet Oil (page 20)

1 tsp Garlic Paste (page 24)

Cooked white rice or tortilla chips, for serving

3 tbsp chopped scallions, for serving

1 tbsp toasted sesame seeds, for serving

1. In a skillet over medium heat, sauté the watermelon cubes for 10 minutes, stirring often. The watermelon will release a lot of liquid, and you'll know it's ready when there is no extra juice at the bottom of the pan. Remove from heat and allow to cool.

2. In a large mixing bowl, combine the soy sauce, pineapple vinegar, lime juice, Scotch bonnet oil, and garlic paste and mix well.

3. Transfer the cooked watermelon to the bowl and toss well to combine. Cover and refrigerate for at least 1 hour to marinate.

4. Serve with cooked white rice or with tortilla chips, topped with the scallions and sesame seeds.

SPICY TOMATO SALAD

Easy, refreshing, spicy, and satisfying—this salad definitely delivers them all!

SERVES: 4   PREP: 10 MIN   COOK: N/A

1. Make the spicy fish sauce: In a small mixing bowl, combine the sugar, garum fish sauce, and pineapple vinegar with 1½ cups warm water. Mix well until the sugar is completely dissolved. Add the garlic paste, Scotch bonnet oil, and lime juice and continue mixing. Chill the sauce in the fridge for about 30 minutes, until cold.

2. Make the tomato salad: In a large bowl, combine the red heirlooms, yellow heirlooms, cucumbers, and red onions. Add 2 tbsp of the chilled spicy fish sauce to the bowl and toss until all ingredients are coated with it.

3. Assemble your plate by arranging the tomatoes and cucumbers first, followed by the red onions, then top with fresh mint and season with black pepper. Serve chilled with the remaining spicy fish sauce on the side for dipping. Store any leftover sauce in an airtight container in the fridge for up to 3 weeks.

SPICY FISH SAUCE

1½ cups granulated sugar

1½ cups Garum Fish Sauce (page 23)

¼ cup Pineapple Vinegar (page 27)

1 tbsp Garlic Paste (page 24)

3 tbsp Scotch Bonnet Oil (page 20)

Juice of 1 lime

TOMATO SALAD

4 red heirloom tomatoes, cut into wedges

1 yellow heirloom tomato, cut into wedges

1 cup sliced English cucumbers

½ cup sliced red onions

2 tbsp chopped fresh mint leaves

Freshly ground black pepper

QUINOA & MANGO SALAD

I used to eat a lot of quinoa when I was trying to diet, but I have to admit, I don't love it. What I do love is mango, so if I put mango on anything, I know I'll eat it! I really focused on the balance of flavors with this recipe.

SERVES: 4   PREP: 5 MIN   COOK: 5 MIN

1 tbsp coconut oil

2 cups chopped spinach

1 cup cooked quinoa

1 cup julienned mangoes

1 tsp salt

COCONUT BASIL DRESSING

Juice of ½ lemon

1 cup full-fat coconut milk

¼ cup fresh Thai basil

1 tbsp Garlic Paste (page 24)

1 tsp Garum Fish Sauce
   (page 23)

1. In a skillet over medium-high heat, melt the coconut oil. Add the chopped spinach and sauté until wilted and bright green, about 2 minutes. Remove from heat and allow to cool.

2. Make the coconut basil dressing: In a blender, combine the lemon juice, coconut milk, Thai basil, garlic paste, and garum fish sauce and pulse until smooth.

3. Add the cooked quinoa and julienned mangoes to the skillet with the spinach and pour in ½ cup of the coconut basil dressing. Stir until combined. Transfer to a bowl and refrigerate until chilled. Store leftover dressing in a small airtight container in the fridge for up to 2 weeks.

4. Serve chilled and enjoy!

NOTE: *For a fresher alternative to this salad (as pictured opposite), skip the skillet. Instead, combine the quinoa, mango and dressing in a bowl and toss with some fresh arugula rather than the cooked spinach.*

GRILLED SHRIMP & MANGO SALAD

Working in the sunshine in Turks, I wanted to create something light, inspired by what was available around me. When I first put this recipe together, I was really excited. Then when I served it and other people loved it, I knew I had hit on something. This is honestly why I cook: making people happy through food.

SERVES: 4   PREP: 15 MIN   COOK: 15 MIN

1. Make the dressing: In a medium bowl, whisk together the coconut milk, lime juice, garlic powder, salt, and curry powder until smooth. Store in an airtight container, and refrigerate for up to 7 days.

2. Preheat your BBQ to high (350°F). Grill the shrimp for 3 minutes per side.

3. Assemble the salad: In a large bowl, combine the shrimp with the mangoes, basil, cilantro, pearl onions, and bell peppers. Drizzle in half of the dressing and lightly fold everything together, adding more dressing as desired. Store any leftover dressing in a small airtight container in the fridge for up to 1 week.

4. Serve with toasted coconut sprinkled on top.

DRESSING

½ cup full-fat coconut milk

2 tbsp lime juice

1 tbsp garlic powder

1 tbsp salt

1 tsp Curry Paste (page 21)

8 to 12 black tiger shrimp, peeled

2 cups sliced mangoes

8 fresh basil leaves

10 fresh cilantro leaves

1 cup thinly sliced red pearl onions or shallots

1 red bell pepper, thinly sliced

¼ cup unsweetened shredded coconut, toasted

Sides

COCONUT MILK BREAD

I collaborated with the Canadian Cancer Society for a campaign called Rise for the Cure. Due to the global pandemic, they weren't able to host their annual walkathon/marathon (which generates a large portion of their much-needed funding for cancer research). Both my mother and grandmother passed from cancer, so I wanted to do whatever I could to help bring awareness. The idea with Rise for the Cure was to get Canadian home bakers of all skill levels to bake virtually with me through social media, and then donate whatever they could to the cause. My grandmother was a big baker, but I never got the chance to bake with her, so this recipe is an homage to her. Essentially, it's a pain au lait with coconut milk, but you can take the base and transform it into any sort of bun or loaf you like—I usually serve a dinner-roll version of it during the holidays and for gatherings. I recommend using it to sop up some jus from my Oxtail Gnocchi (page 201) or for dipping in the Coconut & Corn Soup (page 40).

MAKES: 1 LOAF (10 SLICES)   PREP: 20 MIN + RISING   COOK: 40 MIN

1. Make the starter mix: In a small saucepan over medium heat, combine the flour, coconut milk, and ¼ cup warm water. Stir continuously for 4 to 5 minutes, or until the starter thickens to the consistency of mashed potatoes. Transfer to a bowl and cover with plastic wrap. Let sit until the starter cools to room temperature.

2. Make the final mix: In the bowl of a stand mixer fitted with the paddle attachment, combine all dry ingredients and mix until incorporated.

3. Once mixed, add in the coconut milk, beaten egg, and the starter mix. Using the dough hook attachment, beat on low for 5 minutes.

4. Add the butter and beat for 5 more minutes. Turn the speed up to medium and beat for a final 5 minutes.

5. Transfer the dough to a bowl lightly oiled with coconut oil and cover with plastic wrap. Let sit for 1 hour, or until the dough has doubled in size.

6. Lightly flour your work surface and dump your dough onto it. Divide the dough into three equal pieces. Roll each piece into a log, about 5 to 6 inches long. Braid the logs, pinching the ends together and tucking them under each end to seal.

7. Place the braid horizontally in a 5 × 9-inch bread loaf tin greased with coconut oil. Cover with a kitchen towel and let rise for 45 minutes. Thirty minutes before the second rise is complete, preheat your oven to 375°F.

8. Once the loaf is done rising, baste with coconut oil and top with the shredded coconut. Bake for 40 minutes, or until golden brown. You may need to rotate your pan halfway through the bake if you see the bread coloring on one side more than the other.

9. Remove from the oven and let cool for 15 minutes before removing the bread from the pan. Let cool completely on a cooling rack. Serve and enjoy!

STARTER MIX

¼ cup unbleached organic flour (I use Stone Milled Organic Prairie Hard Red)

¼ cup full-fat coconut milk

FINAL MIX

2½ cups unbleached organic flour

¼ cup granulated sugar

2¼ tsp active dry yeast

1 tsp salt

½ cup full-fat coconut milk, room temperature

1 egg, beaten, room temperature

¼ cup unsalted butter, softened

Coconut oil, for greasing the bowl and pan, and for basting

1 cup unsweetened shredded coconut

CASSAVA AU GRATIN

This recipe was inspired by my new-found appreciation for the mighty cassava, a vegetable that can grow in drought conditions and could do wonders for our food system if adopted for everyday use. This gratin goes well with the Jerk-Marinated Chicken Coq au Vin (page 186) and Coffee-Crusted Steak (page 198).

SERVES: 12   PREP: 15 MIN   COOK: 1HR 15 MIN

2⅓ lb cassava

2 tbsp coconut oil

1 small onion, finely chopped

2 tbsp all-purpose flour

2 cups full-fat coconut milk

1 tsp Garlic Paste (page 24)

1 tsp smoked paprika

2 tbsp chopped fresh flat-leaf parsley

1 cup shredded sharp cheddar

1 cup freshly grated Parmesan

1. Preheat the oven to 350°F.

2. Peel and wash the cassava, and slice lengthwise into ¼-inch-thick slices. Set aside.

3. Melt the coconut oil in a saucepan over medium-high heat. Add the onions and sauté until tender, about 5 minutes.

4. Sprinkle in the flour and continue to cook, stirring continuously. Add the coconut milk and bring to a boil, then reduce to a simmer. Add the garlic paste, paprika, and parsley, mix well, then remove from heat. Add the cheddar and Parmesan and continue to stir.

5. Arrange the cassava slices in a cast-iron skillet, fanning out a handful at a time and placing them in at an angle (this ensures that every scoop will have tender cassava from the bottom and crisp edges from the top). Tuck smaller cassava slices into any gaps to fill them. Pour the coconut milk mixture over the cassava and cover the skillet tightly with aluminum foil.

6. Bake in the oven until tender and creamy, about 45 minutes. Remove the foil and continue baking, uncovered, for an additional 15 minutes. Remove from the oven and allow to cool for 10 minutes before serving.

WHIPPED PROVISIONS

I used to do a lot of pop-up dinners, and I always tried to come up with innovative ways for people to eat African foods, like fufu, a dough made from boiled and mashed ground provisions like plantains and cassava. My version is made with sweet potatoes, plantains, and coconut milk and is served like a mash.

SERVES: 6 TO 8   PREP: 15 MIN   COOK: 30 MIN

4 medium Jamaican sweet potatoes, cubed

2 ripe yellow plantains, cubed

2 tbsp unsalted butter

1 tbsp Garlic Paste (page 24)

¼ cup full-fat coconut milk

½ tsp salt

2 tbsp chopped fresh thyme

Ground cinnamon, to taste

Fresh flat-leaf parsley or scallions, chopped (optional)

Photo on page 106

1. Fill a large stockpot or Dutch oven with 2 inches of water and set over medium-high heat. Set a steamer basket inside and bring the water to a boil.

2. Fill the steamer basket with the sweet potatoes and plantains and cover. Reduce the heat to medium and cook for 20 to 25 minutes, or until potatoes are fork-tender.

3. Meanwhile, in a saucepan set over medium heat, melt the butter. Add the garlic paste and cook until fragrant, 1 to 2 minutes. Add the coconut milk and salt and continue cooking for 5 more minutes, then cover and remove from heat.

4. Drain the provisions from the water, then pour them directly into the saucepan. Return to the stovetop over high heat and cook for 1 minute to allow any excess moisture to evaporate.

5. Set up your stand mixer with the whisk attachment. To the mixing bowl, add the provisions and the thyme and cinnamon. With the mixer running on medium speed, slowly add the warm butter and coconut milk mixture until fully incorporated.

6. Whisk on medium-high speed until the provisions are light and fluffy, 1 to 2 minutes.

7. Let the provisions stand for 5 minutes before transferring to a serving dish. Garnish with freshly chopped parsley or scallions, if desired.

COCONUT MILK MASH

This is basically mashed potatoes with coconut milk. I came up with it one day when I was working a pop-up and we ran out of coconut rice. We had a bunch of potatoes, so, on the fly, I made a coconut milk mash and everyone loved it!

SERVES: 4   PREP: 8 MIN   COOK: 15 MIN

1. Bring a large pot of water to a boil. Reduce heat to medium for a lightly rolling boil. Add the salt and stir continuously until the salt is dissolved.

2. Add the potatoes and cook for 10 minutes, or until they are easily pierced with a fork or paring knife. Drain and allow to cool slightly.

3. Transfer the warm potatoes to a large mixing bowl and mash. Add the coconut cream and, using a whisk, continue mashing until they reach a smooth consistency.

4. Taste and adjust the seasoning to your preference. Serve warm garnished with scallions, if desired, and a good amount of freshly ground black pepper.

¼ tsp salt

1 lb medium white potatoes, peeled and cut into ½- to ¾-inch cubes

1 cup full-fat coconut milk

Chopped scallions (optional)

Freshly ground black pepper

Photo on page 107

WHIPPED PROVISIONS, PAGE 104

COCONUT MILK MASH, PAGE 105

RICE AND PEAS

Rice and peas is a must-have with every meal in Afro-Caribbean cuisine. Some plates might have jerk chicken or escovitch fish, others might have curry goat, but all of them will have rice and peas (as we call the dish in Jamaica, or "peas and rice" as other islands call it). Between the starch of the rice and the protein of the peas, it fills you up for a long time—and it's delicious. Good rice and peas should make any dish it's served with better, but also be tasty enough to eat on its own.

Of all the dishes I've tried to master during my career, rice and peas has given me the most trouble. Part of why I've had such a hard time is that everyone makes it differently. There are countless ways to make it, and everyone thinks their way is best. The "peas" are either pigeon peas, red kidney beans, black eyed peas, or even pinto beans, and the rice can range from long grain to jasmine. The common factor is always coconut milk, and tons of herbs and spices.

The three main things you should pay attention to when making rice and peas are: the cook on the rice, the cook on the peas, and the seasoning. Making sure the rice and the peas are both cooked to their ideal doneness is tricky, because they don't cook at the same time—you have to be careful with the heat. The seasoning (for the Jamaican version) is a mixture of allspice, and Scotch bonnet to bring that signature island flavor. Eventually, I did figure out my own rice and peas recipe, and of course I think it's the best. But I'm not quite ready to share it—yet. In the meantime, try this awesome Okra Pilaf (opposite).

OKRA PILAF

While in Turks and Caicos, I noticed that a lot of Haitians working there threw okra into their peas and rice. I started messing around with that idea, and then they told me how they make it. They use pig tails to give the rice a nice pork flavor, but I swapped them out for guanciale. The liquid released from the okra when cooking helps give this dish a creamy texture and a boost of color.

SERVES: 4 TO 6   PREP: 10 MIN   COOK: 35 MIN

1. Place the diced guanciale in a stockpot and ensure it covers the bottom of the pot completely. Cook on high heat until it is crispy. Remove with a slotted spoon and reserve on a plate lined with paper towel to soak up any excess fat.

2. Add the onions, celery, and peppers to the pot and sauté over high heat until the onions are translucent, about 5 minutes. Add the okra, tomatoes, and rice, mix well, and cook for 3 to 5 minutes so the rice grains are toasted and the vegetables become a little caramelized.

3. Add the garlic paste, Scotch bonnet paste, black-eyed peas, thyme leaves, and pepper, then deglaze the pot with chicken stock.

4. Stir in the coconut milk, cover, and bring to a boil. Reduce the heat to maintain a low simmer and cook until the rice is done, about 20 minutes.

5. Fluff up the rice with a fork and stir in the crispy guanciale. Serve warm.

4 oz guanciale, diced

1 cup chopped onions

½ cup chopped celery

½ cup chopped green bell peppers

2 cups sliced okra (sliced into ½- to ¾-inch-thick disks)

½ cup canned diced tomatoes

2 cups long-grain rice, rinsed and drained

2 tbsp Garlic Paste (page 24)

1 tbsp Scotch Bonnet Paste (page 21)

1 cup black-eyed peas, drained

4 sprigs fresh thyme, leaves only

½ tsp freshly ground black pepper

2 cups chicken stock

2 cups full-fat coconut milk

Photo on page 110

OKRA PILAF, PAGE 109

SALTED COD FRIED RICE

Salt cod is a big part of the Afro-Caribbean diet. While in Turks I was really craving Chinese food, but there wasn't any, so I had to figure out something with the ingredients on hand. I had salted cod and everything to make fried rice, and so my version of Caribbean fried rice was born.

SERVES: 4   PREP: 15 MIN   COOK: 10 MIN

1 tbsp unsalted butter

1 egg

1 cup medium-diced onions

1 cup medium-diced tomatoes

½ cup cubed carrots

½ cup green peas

1 tsp Scotch Bonnet Paste
   (page 21)

1 cup soaked and shredded
   salted cod

3 cups cooked rice, chilled

½ tsp sazón

½ tsp coconut oil

1 tbsp Knorr calamansi liquid
   seasoning (optional)

Chopped scallions, for serving

Freshly ground black pepper,
   to taste

1. Heat a large skillet (cast iron works great) on medium-high heat. Melt the butter in the pan, then crack in the egg and scramble it, breaking it into small pieces as you go. Transfer to a plate and set aside.

2. Return the pan to the heat and sauté the onions, tomatoes, carrots, peas, and Scotch bonnet paste until the vegetables are soft and cooked, about 5 minutes.

3. Turn up the heat to high and add the salted cod. Mix well and cook until all the liquid has reduced.

4. Add the chilled rice, sazón, and Knorr calamansi liquid seasoning (if using) and stir to combine with the fish and veggies. Continue sautéing the rice, stirring every 15 to 20 seconds or so, for 3 minutes, or until you notice the rice and veggies starting to brown slightly and become crispy.

5. Stir in your scrambled egg, give the rice a taste, and adjust the seasoning with black pepper if necessary.

6. Remove from heat, plate up, and serve! Add scallions to garnish, for that extra kick of allium!

TRINIDADIAN CORN PIE

Not to be confused with Jamaican tun cawnmeal or Bajan cou cou, this dish has slowly become a favorite of mine, and Trinidad's second-greatest export (soca being the first). On the island, it's usually eaten as a side during Sunday dinners, and this recipe has the potential to rival any casserole dish that you have in your rotation. Every time I've tried to explain it, I never seem to find the right words . . . it's creamy, salty, cheesy, and spicy—but so much more. And that's how good this dish is: it leaves you at a loss for words.

SERVES: 4   PREP: 15 MIN   COOK: 55 MIN

1. Preheat the oven to 350°F.

2. In a mixing bowl, combine the egg and cornmeal with 1 cup water and whisk together. Set aside.

3. In a skillet over medium-high heat, melt the coconut oil. Add the scallions, onions, bell peppers, salt, and pepper and stir for 2 to 3 minutes, until onions and peppers start to soften.

4. Add the coconut cream and bring to a boil, then quickly add the premixed cornmeal and egg mixture. Reduce the heat to low and cook for about 4 minutes, stirring frequently to avoid any burning.

5. Add the corn and continue cooking, stirring frequently, for another 5 minutes, until the mixture easily comes away from the sides of the skillet.

6. Add ½ cup cheddar and the parsley, Scotch bonnet paste, and sugar and mix well.

7. Top with the remaining cheese and bake until the top is lightly browned and the cheese is bubbly, 30 to 40 minutes. Serve as a side dish or by itself.

1 large egg

½ cup fine cornmeal

4 tbsp coconut oil

2 scallions, chopped

½ cup diced onions

½ cup diced red bell peppers

1 tsp salt

White pepper, to taste

1 cup coconut cream

1 cup canned corn kernels

1 cup shredded sharp cheddar

2 tbsp chopped fresh flat-leaf parsley

½ tsp Scotch Bonnet Paste (page 21)

2 tbsp brown sugar

CORN SALSA

I've been making this salsa for a while, and everyone loves it. It's one of my go-tos, especially for taco night. It's great as a side dish, on top of proteins, or, of course, with tacos!

SERVES: 4   PREP: 10 MIN   COOK: 5 MIN

4 cobs fresh corn

½ cup diced red onions

½ cup chopped scallions

½ cup chopped tomatoes

⅓ cup chopped fresh cilantro, including tender stems

1 tsp Garlic Paste (page 24)

1 tbsp Scotch Bonnet Oil (page 20)

2 tbsp lime juice

1 tsp salt

1. Preheat the broiler.

2. Husk the corn, cut or break each cob into two pieces, and place in a cast-iron skillet. Broil for 5 minutes. Remove from the oven and allow to cool.

3. Use a sharp chef's knife to cut the kernels away from the cobs.

4. Place the corn kernels, along with the rest of the ingredients, in a mixing bowl. Toss everything together to combine. Serve at room temperature. Store any leftovers in an airtight container in the fridge for up to 3 days.

CHARRED CARROTS

My girlfriend isn't a huge fan of vegetables, so I need to sneak them in. One day I threw some carrots in the oven, charred them, and brought out their bitter flavor, which I really loved. Then I paired them with this syrupy sweet-spicy glaze, along with the punchy freshness of a gremolata, which she did. This dish hits all the flavor notes, so it's a guaranteed crowd-pleaser for vegetable lovers and non-vegetable lovers alike.

SERVES: 4   PREP: 10 MIN   COOK: 20 MIN

1. Preheat the oven to 500°F.

2. Prepare the carrots: In a bowl, combine the coconut oil, salt, maple syrup, pepper, and Scotch bonnet oil and mix well. Add the carrots and toss to coat.

3. Arrange the carrots on a baking sheet in one even layer.

4. Roast in the oven for 10 minutes. Remove from the oven and stir well, then redistribute carrots into an even layer and return to the oven for another 5 to 8 minutes, until tender and charred.

5. While the carrots are roasting, make the gremolata: Place the scallions, parsley, garlic paste, and lemon zest in a food processor and pulse until chopped. Add the oil, salt and pepper, and lemon juice. Pulse again until uniformly combined but not too smooth. Taste and adjust seasoning, adding more oil if needed for a looser consistency.

6. Arrange the charred carrots on a serving platter with lemon wedges, if desired, and garnish with gremolata.

CARROTS

1 tbsp coconut oil

1 tsp salt

¼ cup maple syrup

¼ tsp freshly ground black pepper

1 tsp Scotch Bonnet Oil (page 20)

1½ lb heirloom carrots, cut from end to end on the diagonal

Lemon wedges (optional)

GREMOLATA

2 cups chopped scallions

½ cup packed fresh flat-leaf parsley, including tender stems

1 tbsp Garlic Paste (page 24)

Zest and juice of 1 lemon

½ cup olive oil

Salt and freshly ground black pepper, to taste

STEAMED CABBAGE

A very common side dish in Jamaica and the Caribbean, steamed cabbage is often served alongside a protein and peas and rice or ground provisions. It was also one of my mother's favorite things to eat, so it holds a special place in my heart.

SERVES: 6   PREP: 20 MIN   COOK: 20 MIN

1 head green cabbage

2 tbsp salted butter

½ cup sliced red onions

½ cup chopped scallions

½ cup chopped tomatoes

1 tsp Garlic Paste (page 24)

1 tbsp Scotch Bonnet Oil (page 20)

2 tbsp granulated sugar

2 sprigs fresh thyme

1 cup shredded carrots

¼ cup Pineapple Vinegar (page 27)

Salt, to taste

1. Peel the tough outer leaves from the cabbage, remove the core, and shred the cabbage.

2. In a skillet over medium heat, melt the butter. Add the onions and shredded cabbage and increase the heat to high. Add the scallions, tomatoes, garlic paste, and Scotch bonnet oil and cook, stirring often, until the vegetables have softened, about 5 minutes.

3. Sprinkle on the sugar, then add the thyme and carrots, mixing until thoroughly combined.

4. Stir in the pineapple vinegar, cover the skillet, turn off the heat and allow the mixture to steam for 8 minutes. Season with salt and serve.

Vegetable Mains

CONFIT MUSHROOM PIZZA

I truly love and adore the texture and umami flavor that mushrooms can add to a dish, so much so that I am dedicating a whole pizza to the object of my adoration. This one's for the fungis and gals!

SERVES: 4   PREP: 20 MIN   COOK: 20 MIN

1. Make the pizza dough: In a bowl, combine 1 cup warm water, the yeast, and the sugar. Let stand until the mixture foams on top, about 5 minutes.

2. In a stand mixer fitted with the paddle attachment or the dough hook, combine the flour and salt on low speed. Increase the speed to medium, add the yeast mixture, and beat until a soft ball forms.

3. Lightly flour your work surface. Remove the dough from the bowl and knead for a few minutes.

4. Transfer to a lightly oiled bowl and cover with a clean cloth. Let the dough rise for about 30 minutes in a warm, draft-free area.

5. Preheat the oven to 500°F.

6. Make the cashew cream: In a blender, combine the cashew or almond beverage, cashews, nutritional yeast, and garlic paste and pulse until smooth. Set aside.

7. Prepare the toppings: In a large skillet over medium heat, melt the coconut oil. Add the confit mushrooms, onions, and garlic paste. Sauté until all the liquid has evaporated, about 7 to 10 minutes. Remove from heat.

8. On a lightly floured surface, stretch (don't roll!) your dough to around 10 to 12 inches in diameter and place on a lightly floured pizza peel or baking sheet.

9. Spread the cashew cream over the dough, then top with the caramelized onion and mushroom mixture.

10. Bake for about 8 minutes. If needed, turn the oven to broil for an additional 1 to 2 minutes to brown the top.

11. Drizzle with the herb oil, top with baby arugula, and serve immediately.

NOTE: *With this recipe, you can make one big pizza or a couple smaller personal-size pizzas instead (as pictured opposite). I love everything onion—the more the better—but some people aren't so keen, so leave them out if you prefer.*

PIZZA DOUGH

1 tsp instant yeast

1 tsp granulated sugar

2 cups all-purpose flour

1 tsp salt

CASHEW CREAM

4 cups cashew or almond beverage

½ cup unsalted cashews, soaked overnight

¼ cup nutritional yeast

1 tbsp Garlic Paste (page 24)

TOPPINGS

1 tbsp coconut oil

2 cups Confit Mushrooms (page 27)

1 white onion, sliced (optional)

1 tbsp Garlic Paste (page 24)

1 tbsp Herb Oil (page 26)

2 cups baby arugula

MUSHROOM PASTA

This recipe got me through a very dark time. Three months into the global pandemic, there seemed to be no end in sight to the continuous lockdowns happening in Toronto. I was very much lacking inspiration and motivation to work on this book. I've found that whenever I'm feeling down, I can always count on comfort food to lift my spirits. A bowl of oxtail stew usually gets the job done, but due to the COVID-19 restrictions, I wasn't able to leave my home to shop for those ingredients. I skimmed through my fridge instead and threw some ingredients together to create this amazing plant-based pasta. I posted the recipe on social media and it has garnered over 20,000 views! Seeing how well this dish was received reignited the fire in my soul and showed me that there is always light at the end of the tunnel.

SERVES: 4   PREP: 5 MIN   COOK: 10 MIN

CASHEW CREAM

4 cups cashew beverage

1½ cups unsalted cashews, soaked overnight

¼ cup nutritional yeast

1 tbsp Garlic Paste (page 24)

9 oz pappardelle, fettucine, or your favorite pasta

1 tbsp Herb Oil (page 26)

4 cups Confit Mushrooms (page 27)

¼ cup chopped fresh flat-leaf parsley

Salt, to taste

1. Make the cashew cream: In a blender, combine the cashew beverage, cashews, nutritional yeast, and garlic paste and pulse until smooth. The cashew cream can be stored in an airtight container in the fridge for up to 1 week.

2. Cook the pasta according to package instructions.

3. In a cast-iron skillet or sauté pan over high heat, heat the herb oil. Add the cooked pasta and confit mushrooms and mix well. Fold in 1 cup of the cashew cream and the chopped parsley and bring to a light simmer.

4. Remove from heat, adjust the seasoning with salt and more nutritional yeast if desired, and serve.

MUSHROOM WELLINGTON

I've never been a fan of Beef Wellington, so I decided to develop a recipe that started with the same idea but then took it in a new, plant-based direction.

SERVES: 6   PREP: 15 MIN   COOK: 50 MIN

1. In a cast-iron skillet over high heat, melt the coconut oil. Add the onions, garlic paste, and umami paste and cook until the onions become translucent, about 5 minutes.

2. Deglaze the pan with the red wine, then add the confit mushrooms.

3. Sauté on medium heat until all the liquid has cooked off. (This step is crucial. You absolutely do not want any excess liquid in your filling, as it will affect how your Wellington bakes.) Remove from heat and let cool.

4. In a food processor, combine the walnuts, truffle oil, chèvre, and half of your cooled mushroom mixture. Pulse gently for 5 seconds, until the mixture comes together.

5. Add this pulsed mixture back to the skillet, season with salt and pepper, and mix well. Make sure the filling has fully cooled before assembling the Wellington.

6. Preheat your oven to 400°F.

7. Carefully unroll the puff pastry sheets onto a parchment-lined baking sheet. Spread half the mushroom filling along the center of one sheet and, working quickly, roll the pastry up and turn it over so it is seam side down on the baking sheet. Repeat with the second pastry sheet and the other half of the filling.

8. Brush the pastry all over with the beaten egg, then use a sharp chef's knife to score the top of the pastry with your choice of design.

9. Place the baking sheet on the middle rack of the oven and bake for 35 minutes; at the 20-minute mark, rotate the pan for even browning. Let the pastry bake until it is a really deep golden color; this will ensure it is cooked all the way through and the pastry is nice and flaky.

10. Cool for 10 minutes before cutting and serving.

1 tbsp coconut oil

1 large onion, chopped

1 tbsp Garlic Paste (page 24)

1 tbsp Umami Paste (page 25)

¼ cup red wine

2 cups sliced Confit Mushrooms (page 27)

1 cup walnuts

½ tsp truffle oil

1 cup chèvre

Salt and freshly ground black pepper, to taste

2 sheets frozen puff pastry, thawed

1 egg, beaten

CALLALOO CARBONARA

In the Afro-Caribbean community, this creamy callaloo sauce is usually served with crab and dumplings, but I always thought it would work well as a base for a pasta dish. It turns out I was right.

SERVES: 4   PREP: 10 MIN   COOK: 30 MIN

14 oz spaghettini

1 tbsp coconut oil

2 oz prosciutto, cut into ½-inch-wide strips

1 large white onion, chopped

4 cups chopped canned callaloo (amaranth)

8 large okra pods, chopped

2 tbsp Garlic Paste (page 24)

2 cups full-fat coconut milk

1¼ cups freshly grated Parmesan, plus more for serving (optional)

Salt and freshly ground black pepper, to taste

1. In a large pot, bring 8 cups water to a boil. Add the spaghettini and cook according to package instructions.

2. While the pasta is cooking, in a large cast-iron skillet over medium heat, melt the coconut oil. Add the prosciutto and cook, stirring occasionally, until crisp, about 6 minutes. Remove and reserve for garnishing later.

3. Add the onions, callaloo, okra, and garlic paste to the skillet and sauté until the onions are translucent, about 5 minutes. Deglaze the skillet with coconut milk and mix very well.

4. Remove from heat, transfer the mixture to a blender, and purée until smooth.

5. Transfer the mixture to a large frying pan over medium-low heat. Gradually add the Parmesan while stirring to avoid forming any lumps. Add the cooked pasta and toss to ensure the noodles are coated evenly. Season with salt and pepper.

6. Plate your pasta and garnish with the crumbled crispy prosciutto and more Parmesan if desired.

COCONUT & CALLALOO RISOTTO

I wanted to learn more about ancestral foods, so I spent the summer of 2019 at the Black Creek Community Farm with some chef friends and colleagues. This is where I discovered that callaloo was being grown in Ontario but was purchased only by the Asian community and a few restaurants. Callaloo, the dish, is very popular in Jamaica, especially among the Rastafarian community. It is more commonly known in North America as purple amaranth or "pigweed" because it is used to feed livestock on a lot of farms. With this recipe I set out to highlight how delicious the humble leaves of the taro plant can be.

SERVES: 4 TO 6   PREP: 15 MIN   COOK: 30 MIN

1. In a medium saucepan over high heat, heat the vegetable stock until steamy, then lower the heat and keep warm.

2. In a wide saucepan on medium-high heat, melt 4 tbsp of the butter. Add the onions and cook until translucent, about 5 minutes. Add the garlic paste, Italian seasoning, and nutmeg and cook for 30 seconds more.

3. Add the rice and toss to coat with the butter and onions. Let cook until the grains are translucent around the edges and beginning to color, 2 to 3 minutes.

4. Add the white wine and stir it into the rice. Simmer and stir until the wine is almost completely boiled away or absorbed by the rice. Add the callaloo and coconut milk and bring to a simmer.

5. Begin to add the warmed vegetable stock, a ladleful (about ½ cup) at a time. After each addition of stock, stir the rice and do not add another ladleful until the liquid in the pot has been almost all absorbed by the rice. The risotto is ready when it is al dente—cooked through but still a little chewy to the bite—and the callaloo is tender.

6. When the risotto is ready, finish by stirring in the remaining 1 tbsp butter, the Parmesan, and the lemon juice. Season with salt and pepper to taste.

4 cups vegetable stock

5 tbsp unsalted butter

1 cup chopped onions

2 tbsp Garlic Paste (page 24)

½ tsp Italian seasoning

⅛ tsp ground nutmeg

2 cups risotto rice (I use arborio)

½ cup white wine

1 cup chopped canned callaloo

1 cup full-fat coconut milk

¾ cup finely grated Parmesan

1 tsp lemon juice

Salt and freshly ground black pepper, to taste

MUSHROOM & LIMA BEAN CASSOULET

This dish is inspired by one of my childhood favorites, "franks and beans." When I was a teenager in Jamaica, we would often have potlucks or, as we call them, "run a boat." Our dish would be sliced hot dogs with canned pinto beans and fried dumplings. My palate has gotten more refined since those days, and this recipe is a testament to that.

SERVES: 4   PREP: 10 MIN   COOK: 20 MIN

1 tbsp coconut oil

1 large onion, julienned

1 red bell pepper, julienned

1 medium carrot, diced

3 stalks celery, diced

1 tbsp Garlic Paste (page 24)

2 cups sliced Confit Mushrooms (page 27)

½ cup red wine

1 cup vegetable stock

2 tbsp smoked paprika

1 tbsp Scotch Bonnet Paste (page 21)

4 cups canned lima beans, rinsed and drained

Salt and freshly ground black pepper, to taste

Crusty bread, for serving

1. In a cast-iron skillet over high heat, melt the coconut oil. Add the onions, peppers, carrots, celery, and garlic paste and cook until the onions become translucent, about 5 minutes. Add the sliced confit mushrooms and mix well.

2. Deglaze the pan with the red wine, then add the beef stock and bring to a boil.

3. Add the smoked paprika, Scotch bonnet paste, and lima beans and stir to incorporate. Continue cooking on high heat until the liquid has reduced and the sauce becomes thick.

4. Check your seasoning and adjust to your taste, then remove from heat. Serve hot with some crusty bread.

LENTIL RAGU

This ragu was one of the first Rastafarian or "Ital" recipes I was introduced to. I would often indulge in some Ital lasagna from this Afro-Caribbean plant-based restaurant in Kensington Market in Toronto, and out of sheer curiosity, I tried to replicate it. It worked out really well and became my go-to for Meatless Mondays.

SERVES: 4   PREP: 18 MIN   COOK: 1½ HR

1. In a large saucepan over high heat, melt the coconut oil. Add the onions, carrots, celery, and garlic paste. Lower the heat and cook gently for 15 to 20 minutes, until everything is softened and the onions are translucent.

2. Stir in the lentils, chopped tomatoes, tomato paste, thyme, and vegetable stock. Bring to a simmer and cook for about 50 minutes, until the lentils are tender, stirring periodically to avoid anything burning or sticking to the bottom of the pan.

3. Stir in the Scotch bonnet paste at the end for a kick, and season with salt and pepper. Serve with white rice or spaghetti.

1 tbsp coconut oil

2 cups chopped onions

3 cups chopped carrots

3 stalks celery, chopped

2 tbsp Garlic Paste (page 24)

2 cups canned red lentils, rinsed and drained

4 cups canned chopped tomatoes

2 tbsp tomato paste

1 tbsp fresh thyme leaves

4 cups vegetable stock

1 tbsp Scotch Bonnet Paste (page 21)

Salt and freshly ground black pepper, to taste

Cooked white rice or spaghetti, for serving

SMOKY MUSHROOM STEW

A vegetarian play on a Hungarian goulash, this is one of the many recipes that have helped me reduce my animal-protein consumption. Whenever I'm in my kitchen cooking, I often ask myself two questions: Is it good for me? Is it good for the environment? This dish is undoubtedly a yes to both.

SERVES: 4   PREP: 20 MIN   COOK: 35 MIN

1 tbsp coconut oil

1 large onion, chopped

2 red bell peppers, chopped

1 tbsp Garlic Paste (page 24)

1 (14 oz) can crushed tomatoes

1 tbsp tomato paste

1 tbsp Scotch Bonnet Paste (page 21)

2 tbsp smoked paprika

2 cups vegetable stock

2 cups Confit Mushrooms (page 27)

Salt and freshly ground black pepper, to taste

Cooked noodles, for serving

Sour cream, for serving

1. In a cast-iron skillet over high heat, melt the coconut oil. Add the onions, peppers, and garlic paste and cook until the onions become translucent, about 5 minutes.

2. Add the crushed tomatoes, tomato paste, Scotch bonnet paste, and smoked paprika and mix well. Add the vegetable stock and bring to a boil. Lower the heat, cover, and simmer gently for 25 minutes.

3. Remove the lid and fold in the confit mushrooms, then continue cooking for an additional 5 minutes to deepen the flavor. Season to taste.

4. Serve over noodles with a dollop of sour cream.

RED KIDNEY BEAN STEW

As much as death and taxes are certainties in life, so is "Soup Saturday" in Jamaican households. This dish is a true staple in Jamaican cuisine, and can be served as a soup or stew with white rice and my Spicy Tomato Salad (page 93). I removed the animal protein to make it more plant-forward and opted for the stew version here.

SERVES: 6   PREP: 20 MIN   COOK: 1 HR 40 MIN

1. Make the stew: Place the soaked red kidney beans in a large saucepan, cover with water, and bring to a boil. Lower the heat to a simmer and cook until tender, about 1 hour.

2. Drain the beans and add them back to the saucepan (discarding the cooking water). Add the vegetable stock, coconut milk, onions, carrots, garlic paste, Scotch bonnet paste, and ginger. Simmer for another 30 minutes, or until the sauce is thick. Season with salt and pepper, to taste.

3. Make the dumpling spinners: In a bowl, combine the flour and salt, add ¼ cup cold water, and mix to make a stiff dough. Pinch off about 1 tablespoon of dough and roll it between the palms of your hands to form a softly tapered cylindrical spinner shape. Repeat until all the dough has been shaped into spinners.

4. Add the spinners to the simmering stew and cook for 7 minutes; the spinners are ready when they begin to float (they are not visible in the photo opposite).

5. Serve the stew over white rice and enjoy!

STEW

2 cups dried red kidney beans, soaked overnight

6 cups vegetable stock

2 cups full-fat coconut milk

1 large onion, diced

1 medium carrot, diced

1 tbsp Garlic Paste (page 24)

1 tbsp Scotch Bonnet Paste (page 21)

1 tbsp ground ginger

Salt and freshly ground black pepper, to taste

DUMPLING SPINNERS

½ cup all-purpose flour

¼ tsp salt

Cooked white rice, for serving

PLANTAIN FRITTATA

As a teenager, I spent a lot of time in the kitchen preparing my own breakfast before school. I've been making this frittata for years, long before I even knew what a frittata was! It was just instinctual to add ripe plantains to my morning eggs, and as I got older, the ingredients became more sophisticated and the techniques and preparation more ambitious. To me, this is the ultimate breakfast food, especially if you are a plantain lover.

SERVES: 6   PREP: 15 MIN   COOK: 40 MIN

3 overripe plantains (black skin)

¼ cup vegetable oil

1 tbsp coconut oil

1 medium white onion, chopped

1 green bell pepper, diced

1 cup sliced Confit Mushrooms (page 27)

1 medium plum tomato, chopped

8 large eggs

1 tsp chicken or vegetable bouillon powder

Scotch Bonnet Oil (page 20), for serving

Chopped scallions, for serving

1. Preheat the oven to 350°F.

2. Peel the skin off the plantains, then cut into rounds about ¼ inch thick.

3. In a cast-iron skillet over medium-high heat, heat the vegetable oil. Fry the plantains for 2 to 3 minutes on one side, then flip and cook for 2 to 3 minutes more, until light golden brown. Set aside on a plate lined with paper towel to soak up any excess oil.

4. Discard the vegetable oil and return the skillet to high heat. Melt the coconut oil and then add the onions, peppers, confit mushrooms, and tomatoes and cook until the onions become translucent, 7 to 8 minutes.

5. Crack the eggs into a bowl and beat them together, then season with the bouillon powder.

6. Return the plantains to the skillet and use a spatula to ensure that all your ingredients are spread out evenly in the skillet. Pour the beaten egg mixture into the skillet and turn down the heat to medium-low.

7. Once the eggs start to lightly simmer, place the skillet in the oven and bake for 25 minutes, or until the center firms up.

8. Remove from the oven and let cool for about 8 minutes. Serve still warm, with a drizzle of Scotch bonnet oil and a scattering of scallions.

PLANTAIN PASTELON

Here is another plant-forward version of an Afro-Caribbean staple (that's actually Puerto Rican in origin). It is traditionally served using ground beef or pork, but I wanted to provide a twist for those who are trying to lower their meat consumption, so I used a lentil ragu instead. A pastelon is essentially a lasagna with sheets of fried plantain, rather than pasta noodles, between each layer of ragu. It's a great option for entertaining large groups, and I usually serve it around Thanksgiving and Christmas.

SERVES: 6   **PREP: 15 MIN**   **COOK: 1½ HR**

1. Preheat the oven to 350°F.

2. Use a knife to cut off both ends of the plantains. Take the tip of your knife and cut a slit down the back of each plantain, then peel as you would a banana. Carefully running the knife down the length of the plantain, slice each plantain into ⅛- to ¼-inch-thick long slabs.

3. In a large skillet over medium heat, heat the vegetable oil. Add four to five slices of plantain to the oil, making sure not to crowd the pan. Fry the plantains for 2 minutes, then, using tongs, carefully flip the plantain slices over in the pan and cook for 2 more minutes, until golden brown. Remove from the pan and place on a baking sheet lined with paper towel to soak up any excess oil. Repeat until all plantain slices have been fried to golden-brown perfection.

4. Take a 9 × 13-inch baking dish and create a base layer of plantain slices in the bottom. Follow up with a layer of lentil ragu (about ½ cup) and then a layer of mozzarella (about ¼ cup). Continue layering the plantains, lentil ragu, and mozzarella until all the ingredients have been used up, with the mozzarella on top.

5. Cover your baking dish with aluminum foil and bake for 45 minutes. Remove the foil and continue baking, uncovered, for 10 to 15 minutes more, or until the mozzarella is bubbly and a bit crispy.

6. Serve with slices of ripe avocado, a scattering of parsley, and a lime wedge.

6 ripe yellow plantains

1 cup vegetable oil

4 cups Lentil Ragu (page 137)

2 cups shredded mozzarella

Ripe avocado, sliced, for serving

Lime wedges, for serving

Chopped flat-leaf parsley, for serving

ZUCCHINI BOATS

I like to think of these boats as the perfect vessel to take you to flavor town. This dish is one of my favorites when I'm watching my weight, as it never feels like I'm depriving myself of good food.

SERVES: 2   PREP: 8 MIN   COOK: 15 MIN

3 medium zucchinis

1 tbsp coconut oil, melted

Salt and freshly ground black pepper, to taste

1½ cups Lentil Ragu (page 137)

1 cup coarsely shredded pepper jack cheese

½ cup chopped fresh cilantro, for serving

1. Place a rimmed baking sheet in the oven and heat the oven to 450°F.

2. Cut the zucchinis in half lengthwise. Using a teaspoon, hollow out each zucchini half. Brush the cut sides of each zucchini half with coconut oil, then place on the heated baking sheet, cut side down. Roast for 5 minutes.

3. Turn the zucchini halves cut side up and season with salt and pepper. Divide the lentil ragu among the zucchini halves (about ¼ cup per half) and top with shredded cheese. Continue roasting until the zucchinis are just tender and the cheese has melted and become bubbly, 8 to 10 minutes.

4. Remove from the oven, garnish with chopped cilantro, and serve.

ITAL

Ital cooking—"vital," but dropping the "v"—is a Rastafarian approach to food that focuses on plant-based, natural foods, and it is one of the most exciting parts of Afro-Caribbean cuisine. I've spent a lot of time researching Ital, and I still feel like I'm only scratching the surface. Ital food matters to me personally because we turned to its more healthful way of eating when my mom was sick, and because it's connected to Africa (Ethiopia, specifically) through its Rastafarian roots. It promotes a model of eating that allows for sustainability and food sovereignty with the community.

The Ital diet is part of the larger Ital belief system and Rastafarian culture. Rastafarians believe that everything in the world is connected, and how you eat should reflect that too—eating directly from the earth, with foods that are completely natural and unmodified. For me, one of the most challenging aspects of Ital cooking is not using salt. Imagine being a chef taught his whole career that salt is the most important ingredient in the kitchen! With Ital, you must make food taste good without salt. Ital chefs have so many ways of bringing out natural flavors that you don't miss the salt. It has a lot to do with the quality of the ingredients used, lots of fresh herbs, and some mystery and wizardry.

There are parts of Ital that I've incorporated into my cooking—you'll see that in the plant-based recipes in this book—but I can't wait to go and spend a few months in the bush learning directly from the masters.

MUSHROOM & BLUEBERRY TORTE

I'm a huge fan of mixing sweet and savory ingredients. As a chef, one of my biggest challenges is creating the perfect balance between ingredients that would normally never be paired together, and that's exactly what I did with this recipe.

SERVES: 6   PREP: 20 MIN   COOK: 1 HR

1. In a saucepan over medium heat, combine the coconut milk, garlic paste, and corn flour and gently heat until simmering but not boiling. Remove from heat.

2. In a mixing bowl, combine the egg, egg yolks, and mascarpone and whisk together. Temper the egg mixture by slowly adding the warm coconut milk mixture while whisking constantly to ensure it stays smooth.

3. Once fully incorporated, transfer back to the saucepan and return the pan to the stove over low heat. Cook for 10 minutes, or until thickened, whisking constantly to prevent the mixture from sticking to the base of the pan.

4. Line an 8-inch springform pan with parchment paper (alternatively, you can use an unlined cast-iron pan). Pour the custard mixture into the pan, then top with the confit mushrooms, Gruyère, and fresh blueberries.

5. Bake for 40 minutes, until the custard mixture has set but still has a slight wobble in the middle. Remove the torte from the oven and let rest and cool for 20 minutes.

6. Carefully remove from the pan. Top with the toasted almond slivers and freshly chopped parsley, then slice and serve.

1½ cups full-fat coconut milk

1 tbsp Garlic Paste (page 24)

2 tbsp corn flour

1 egg

4 egg yolks

14 oz mascarpone, room temperature

1 cup Confit Mushrooms (page 27)

5 oz Gruyère, shredded

1 cup fresh blueberries

1 tbsp slivered almonds, toasted, for serving

Fresh flat-leaf parsley, chopped, for serving

Fish + Seafood

CARIBBEAN-SPICED STEAMED FISH

Banana leaves are an integral part of food preparation in a lot of cuisines. In the Afro-Caribbean community, they can be used for barbecuing, baking, or steaming. The most common use is for a dessert called duckanoo or blue draws, which is essentially a Jamaican tamale.

I drew inspiration from duckanoos for this recipe, using the banana leaf as my vessel and steaming as my cooking method. This method gives your fish a smooth, silky texture and adds a nutty flavor and captivating aroma from the robust smell of the leaves. "Dunckanoo-style" has become my favorite way of preparing fish.

SERVES: 4   PREP: 5 MIN   COOK: 15 TO 20 MIN

1. In a medium saucepan, bring 2 cups water to a rolling boil, then reduce to a simmer.

2. Cut the fish fillets in half vertically and place in a large mixing bowl. Add the canola oil, allspice, salt, pepper flakes, fresh thyme, coriander, cinnamon, ginger, and nutmeg. Using your hands, mix very well to ensure the fillets are all evenly coated.

3. Place three lemon slices, slightly overlapping, in the center of each banana leaf piece. Place one half fish fillet on top of each set of lemon slices. Fold each leaf over on top of the fish to enclose it.

4. Place the packets, folded side down, in a bamboo basket and cover. Place the bamboo basket over the saucepan and steam for 15 minutes.

5. Serve each parcel, open, on a plate with some Peruvian purple potato mash (as pictured opposite), or some Coconut Milk Mash (page 105), Trinidadian Corn Pie (page 115), or Okra Pilaf (page 109).

NOTE: *Alternatively, if you don't have a bamboo basket, preheat the oven to 400°F. Place the packets, folded side down, on a baking sheet. Place a skillet, pan, or steel bowl with 2 cups boiling water on the bottom rack of the oven. Add the baking sheet with the fish packets on the top rack. Bake for 20 minutes, until the water has evaporated.*

2 (6 oz) fish fillets (such as snapper, halibut, or sea bass)

1 tbsp canola oil

1 tsp ground allspice

1 tsp salt

1 tsp crushed red pepper flakes

1 tsp chopped fresh thyme leaves

¼ tsp ground coriander

¼ tsp ground cinnamon

⅛ tsp ground ginger

⅛ tsp ground nutmeg

12 thin lemon slices

4 (12-inch-square) pieces fresh or frozen and thawed banana leaf

HONEY-GLAZED SALMON

A friend of mine makes this harissa salmon dish that I can't get enough of, so I tried my own version, swapping out the harissa for my Scotch bonnet paste. Serve this with rice and it's a quick and easy dinner for the family, ready in 15 minutes flat.

SERVES: 4   PREP: 5 MIN   COOK: 10 MIN

¼ cup honey

2 tbsp Scotch Bonnet Paste (page 21)

2 tbsp coconut oil

2 (6 oz) salmon fillets, skin on, cut in half

Lime wedges (optional), for serving

Chopped flat-leaf parsley, for serving

1. In a mixing bowl, whisk together the honey and Scotch bonnet paste and set aside.

2. Heat a skillet over high heat and melt the coconut oil. Place the salmon in the skillet, skin side up, and cook until opaque on the side being seared, about 3 minutes.

3. Flip the fillets and brush with the honey and Scotch bonnet mixture. Keep cooking for about another 7 minutes, checking the bottom to make sure the skin gets crispy but does not burn. Serve immediately with lime wedges, if desired, and a scattering of parsley or other fresh herb.

YAWDMON BURRITOS

When I was working in catering, I was always trying to come up with new ways to make food interesting. I had a bunch of Caribbean ingredients around me and I wanted to try something different, but super satisfying. Here I use the Honey-Glazed Salmon from page 154 in a new way. What could be better than a Jamaican burrito?

SERVES: 4   PREP: 10 MIN + SOAKING   COOK: 20 MIN

1. Make the coconut rice: Rinse the rice in water until the water runs pretty clear. Drain, then soak the rice in water for 15 minutes. Drain again.

2. In a small saucepan over medium-high heat, combine the rice, coconut milk, ½ cup water, sugar, garlic paste, and salt. Bring to a simmer so the entire surface of the liquid is rippling (not just the edges), give it ONE stir (not more!), cover with the lid, and immediately turn the heat down to low. Allow the rice to slowly cook for 14 minutes. Remove from heat and let rest, undisturbed, for 10 minutes.

3. Make the burritos: Using a fork, shred the cooked salmon fillets.

4. Spread about ½ cup red kidney bean purée on each tortilla, then add 1 cup coconut rice in the center of each. Top each with ½ cup shredded salmon, ½ cup cabbage, ¼ cup corn salsa, and a quarter of the sliced avocado.

5. Fold opposite sides (left and right) of each tortilla over the filling, then roll up (bottom to top), burrito-style.

6. Preheat a frying pan over high heat. Place the burritos, seam sides down, in the pan and sear for 1 minute. Flip and sear on the opposite side for 30 seconds. Serve with salsa, sour cream, and lime wedges.

COCONUT RICE

2 cups long-grain white rice

3 cups full-fat coconut milk

1 tbsp granulated sugar

1 tbsp Garlic Paste (page 24)

½ tsp salt

BURRITOS

1 recipe Honey-Glazed Salmon (page 154)

2 cups Red Kidney Bean Purée (page 25)

4 (12-inch) flour tortillas

2 cups shredded purple cabbage

1 cup Corn Salsa (page 116)

1 avocado, pitted and sliced

SERVING

Salsa

Sour cream

Lime wedges

HELLSHIRE FISH TACOS

Hellshire Beach in Jamaica is a hub for tourists, but it's also the epicenter of culinary inspiration for young Jamaican chefs. There are a multitude of beachside restaurant shacks offering a variety of preparations of delicious local seafood that's been spearfished or line-caught that day. You hand-select your seafood from a cooler in the hallway leading to the kitchen, and it's either grilled, steamed in foil, or fried in a cast-iron Dutch oven over an open charcoal fire. One of the most popular methods is escovitch, where the fish is pan-fried then finished with escovitch sauce—a pickled condiment of Scotch bonnets, shaved carrot and onion, and warm vinegar. For this recipe, I wanted to pay homage to Hellshire, giving you the option to choose both your favorite fish and your preferred cooking method: if you don't want to fry it, you can grill or steam it instead—just like on the beach. Given that these are tacos, I've replaced the bammy (which is what you'd get on the beach) with a plantain tortilla, but I've kept the escovitch sauce because it's an integral part of what makes seafood from Hellshire so special.

SERVES: 4   PREP: 15 MIN + RESTING   COOK: 45 MIN

1. Make the tortillas: In a large bowl, combine the flours, baking powder, and salt. Stir in 1½ cups water and the oil. Turn out onto a floured surface and knead 10 to 12 times, adding a little more flour or water if needed to achieve a smooth dough. Let rest, uncovered on the counter, for 10 minutes.

2. Divide the dough into eight portions. On a lightly floured surface, roll each portion into a 7-inch circle. Try putting some parchment paper on top and underneath the dough to stop it sticking to the rolling pin (photos 1 + 2 below).

3. Use the lard or other fat to grease a cast-iron or other heavy skillet, and cook the tortillas over medium heat until lightly browned, about 1 minute on each side. Keep warm in the oven until serving.

CONTINUED

TORTILLAS
3 cups all-purpose flour

1 cup plantain flour

2 tsp baking powder

1 tsp salt

3 cups vegetable oil

2 tbsp lard or any plant- or animal-based fat

SCALLION MAYO
½ cup chopped scallions

Zest of 1 lime

1 tbsp lime juice

1 egg yolk

1 tsp salt

1 cup vegetable oil

GINGER BEER–BATTERED FISH
1 cup all-purpose flour

1 tbsp garlic powder

1 tbsp onion powder

1 tbsp freshly ground black pepper

1 egg, beaten

1 to 1½ cups Jamaican ginger beer

3 cups vegetable oil

1½ lb skinless cod, cut into 1 x 4-inch strips

ESCOVITCH SAUCE

2 tbsp vegetable oil

1 medium red or white onion, cut into small dice or thin strips

1 medium carrot, cut into small dice or thin strips

1 medium green bell pepper, cut into small dice or thin strips

1 tbsp Scotch Bonnet Paste (page 21)

1 tsp ground allspice

2 cups Pineapple Vinegar (page 27)

1 tbsp granulated sugar

Pickled Scotch Bonnets (page 20) (optional)

4. Make the scallion mayo: In a food processor or blender, combine the scallions, lime zest and juice, egg yolk, and salt. Cover and mix for a few seconds. Turn the machine to the lowest speed. With the machine running, add the oil in a thin, steady stream through the opening in the lid. The mayonnaise will emulsify quickly, in less than a minute. If necessary, turn off the processor or blender and scrape down the sides so the blades can reach the ingredients. Store in an airtight container in the fridge for up to 2 weeks.

5. Make the ginger beer-battered fish: In a small mixing bowl, combine the flour, garlic powder, onion powder, black pepper, and beaten egg. Stir in 1 cup of the ginger beer (add a little more, if needed, to get your desired texture).

6. In a deep nonstick skillet over medium-high heat, heat the oil to 350°F.

7. Dip the fish strips into the batter, coating them all over. Drop them, one at a time, into the hot oil. Fry the fish, turning once, until both sides are golden brown. Drain the excess oil on paper towels. Repeat until all the fish is fried.

8. Make the escovitch sauce: In the skillet used to fry the fish, heat the vegetable oil over medium heat. Add the onions, carrots, green peppers, Scotch bonnet paste, and allspice and sauté for 2 minutes. Stir in the vinegar and sugar, bring to a boil, then turn off the heat.

9. Assemble the tacos: Add some battered fish to each warm tortilla, and top with scallion mayo and the escovitch sauce. Serve with sliced pickled scotch bonnet peppers for optional added heat.

NOTE: *On Hellshire Beach you'll often get escovitch sauce in a squeezy bottle, so you squeeze out the concentrated sauce leaving the vegetables in the bottle. I like to serve these tacos with the vegetables too though, so I deconstruct the sauce a bit and add them individually for plating.*

PEPPER SHRIMP PAELLA

My first introduction to the awesome combination of salty and spicy was back in my childhood. My parents were no longer together, but they did a fantastic job of co-parenting, and I relished the weekends when I would go to my dad's "bachelor pad." My father is the kind of man who does anything to put a smile on your face, no matter the cost, so when I asked to go to the beach (a 2-hour drive) and learn to swim, it was no surprise that he said yes. None of the swimming lessons stuck that day, but what did resonate with me were the peppah shrimps sold in see-through plastic bags by roadside vendors. Since the vendors can't keep them refrigerated on the side of the road, these treats are incredibly salty to help preserve them and keep them fresh. They are also so spicy you can still feel your lips tingle from the Scotch bonnet peppers hours after eating. But they pack such a flavorful punch that, no matter how spicy, you can't get enough!

In 2017, I went back to Jamaica to visit my mother's grave, but I also made it my mission to find out from the street vendors what was in the shrimp marinade that would permeate through those plastic bags.

SERVES: 4   PREP: 10 MIN + MARINATING   COOK: 30 MIN

1. Prepare the shrimp: In a bowl, combine the prawns and Scotch bonnet paste and mix well. Let marinate in the fridge for at least 30 minutes.

2. In a cast-iron skillet over high heat, melt the coconut oil. Once the skillet is hot, sear the marinated prawns for 30 seconds on each side, until the color changes to a bright pinkish-orange hue. Remove the prawns from the pan and reserve on a baking sheet lined with parchment paper.

3. Make the rice: Add 2 tbsp more coconut oil to the pan, then add the rice, garlic paste, and turmeric. Stir until all the rice grains are evenly coated in turmeric. Deglaze the pan with white wine, add the bouillon powder and 3½ cups water, and stir. Reduce the heat to medium and simmer until the liquid has reduced by more than half, about 5 minutes.

4. Preheat the oven to 405°F.

5. Add the mixed vegetables, bell peppers, and coconut milk to the pan. Give everything a proper, even mix. Simmer until the liquid has reduced by a third, about 5 minutes. Add the fish sauce and black pepper and mix well.

6. Add the seared prawns back to the pan, positioning them on top of the rice mixture.

7. Place your skillet in the oven and bake for 10 minutes, or until the liquid in the skillet has completely dissolved and the rice is fully cooked. Serve with lemon wedges and sprinkled with cilantro.

SHRIMP

1 lb frozen medium spot prawns (or shrimp), thawed and deveined

3 tbsp Scotch Bonnet Paste (page 21)

2 tbsp coconut oil

RICE

2 tbsp coconut oil

2 cups long-grain white rice, rinsed and drained

1 tbsp Garlic Paste (page 24)

1 tsp ground turmeric

½ cup dry white wine

2 tbsp fish bouillon powder

1½ cups frozen mixed vegetables (green peas, corn, carrots)

⅓ cup chopped red bell peppers

1½ cups full-fat coconut milk

1 tbsp fish sauce

½ tsp freshly ground black pepper

Lemon wedges, for serving

Chopped fresh cilantro, for serving

PEPPER SHRIMP PAELLA, PAGE 161

GINGER MUSSELS

I first tried the Filipino mussel dish Tinolang Tahong when I was in LA. The whole dish was good, but the broth was crazy, with so much ginger and an incredibly flavorful stock that I could drink forever. This is my version. Eat it with your hands: use the mussels to scoop the broth, then drink the rest or sop it all up with some crusty bread.

SERVES: 4   **PREP: 10 MIN**   **COOK: 10 MIN**

1. In a large pot over high heat, melt the coconut oil and sauté the garlic paste, ginger, and onions until the onions are translucent. Add the mussels, then pour in the white wine and seafood stock and bring to a boil. Reduce the heat and simmer, covered, for about 10 minutes.

2. Once the mussel shells are opened, add the cilantro leaves. Simmer for 2 more minutes, then season with salt and pepper. Discard any unopened shells.

3. Serve with crusty bread and enjoy!

1 tbsp coconut oil

1 tbsp Garlic Paste (page 24)

1 thumb-sized piece fresh ginger, grated

1 large red onion, chopped

1 lb mussels, cleaned

½ cup white wine

1 cup seafood stock

1 bunch fresh cilantro, leaves only

Salt and freshly ground black pepper, to taste

Crusty bread, for serving

LOBSTER RUNDOWN

The ingredients for a rundown, also known as run dun or fling-me-far, vary depending on the region of Jamaica where it is being prepared, but the main components are seafood (mackerel and shellfish are common), coconut milk, ground provisions, aromatics, and chili peppers. It is one of those dishes that you can create multiple versions of by adding new and exciting ingredients. I encourage you to use this as your base, but be curious and explore your options!

SERVES: 4   PREP: 10 MIN   COOK: 20 MIN

1 tbsp coconut oil

1 medium onion, chopped

1 medium red bell pepper, medium-diced

1 scallion, chopped

2 tbsp Garlic Paste (page 24)

1 tsp grated fresh ginger

1 tbsp Curry Paste (page 21)

2 tbsp cornstarch

1 cup dry white wine

2 cups full-fat coconut milk

2 whole rock lobsters, raw, deshelled and meat chopped into ½-inch cubes

2 tbsp chopped fresh thyme

Salt and freshly ground black pepper, to taste

Cooked rice, for serving

Chopped fresh flat-leaf parsley or scallions, for serving

1. In a skillet over medium-high heat, melt the coconut oil. Add the onions, peppers, scallions, garlic paste, and ginger and sweat until the onions are translucent, about 5 minutes.

2. Add the curry paste and cornstarch and continue to cook, stirring together until the sauce has thickened.

3. Deglaze the pan with the white wine, then add the coconut milk and continue to stir, ensuring the coconut sauce is smooth and free of clumps.

4. Add the lobster meat and thyme, reduce the heat to a simmer, and let simmer for 5 minutes, until the lobster meat is cooked. Season with salt to taste.

5. Serve over rice, topped with a sprinkle of chopped parsley, and some freshly ground black pepper.

JERK-SPICED SEAFOOD BOIL

In September 2013, I accepted an executive chef position at Rock Lobster Food Company, and I have the chef and owner, Matt Dean Pettit, to thank for helping me rediscover my love of seafood. The restaurant specialized in East Coast Canadian comfort cuisine, and sported a concise lobster-focused menu that took lobster off its white-tablecloth and silver-platter pedestal and into more approachable, casual, high-meets-low dishes instead—such as lobster poutine, lobster mac and cheese, lobster grilled cheese, and lobster corn dogs, to name just a few.

The definitive show-stopper on the menu was the seafood boil. Customers ordered this not just because of the bold flavors and the variety of seafood it contains, but because you had all eyes on you in the dining room as the server walked over with a large 16-quart stockpot wafting herbaceous and aromatic fragrances. Rock Lobster has since closed, but whenever I have large gatherings and don't feel like cooking something laborious (but still want to impress my guests), this jerk take on a seafood boil is my go-to.

SERVES: 4   PREP: 10 MIN   COOK: 35 MIN

1. In a large pot over medium heat, melt the coconut oil. Add the sausages and sear for 2 to 3 minutes on two sides, or until golden brown. Remove from the pot and set aside (no need to clean the pot yet). The sausages will finish cooking later in the recipe.

2. Add 6 cups water and the jerk dry rub, thyme, lemon juice, and potatoes to the pot and bring to a boil. Boil for 8 minutes to infuse the flavors into the broth. Cut the sausages into thirds and return to the pot, add the corn, and boil for 5 minutes.

3. Add the mussels and the lobster tails and rum and boil for 3 minutes. Add the shrimp and boil an additional minute, or until the sausages reach a minimum internal temperature of 160°F, the shrimp are pink, and the lobster tails reach a minimum internal temperature of 145°F.

4. Drain into a colander and discard the broth and remaining thyme sprigs. Discard any mussels with unopened shells. Place the colander onto a clean plate and set on the table. Garnish with a sprinkle of jerk dry rub, some chopped parsley, and a squeeze of lemon. Serve with clarified butter and enjoy family-style.

NOTE: *The ingredients and quantities used in this recipe are super flexible, and it's very easy to scale up for a larger crowd. Add more potatoes and corn for extra bulk, or try some boiled eggs in there for variety, and always lots of sausage. My go-to for the choice of seafood is shrimp, mussels and lobster tails or claws, but you can really tailor it to your personal preference.*

1 tbsp coconut oil

4 spicy Italian sausages

3 tbsp Jerk Dry Rub (page 19), plus more for serving

5 sprigs fresh thyme

Juice of 1 lemon, plus more for serving

1 cup red-skinned potatoes

2 cobs fresh corn, cut in half

1lb mussels, cleaned

2 lobster tails, cut in thirds

2 cups rum

1 cup peeled and deveined shrimp

Fresh flat-leaf parsley, chopped, for serving

¼ cup clarified butter, for serving

SPICY SHRIMP ROLL

When I worked at Rock Lobster Food Company, this was the only recipe of my own that I got on the menu; it's my version of a lobster roll, but with an injection of Caribbean flavor. It's the perfect amount of spice for those who are not into really spicy food.

SERVES: 4   PREP: 5 MIN   COOK: 5 MIN

¼ cup mayonnaise

1 tsp diced fresh ginger

¼ cup chopped fresh flat-leaf parsley

1 tsp Scotch Bonnet Paste (page 21)

1 tsp Garum Fish Sauce (page 23)

Juice of 1 lemon

12 oz peeled and deveined large shrimp, tails removed

2 scallions, finely chopped

⅓ cup chopped roasted red peppers

Freshly ground black pepper

4 split-top hot dog buns

8 small Bibb lettuce leaves (optional)

Potato chips, for serving

Pickles, for serving

1. In a large bowl, whisk together the mayonnaise, ginger, parsley, Scotch bonnet paste, garum fish sauce, and lemon juice.

2. Bring a large saucepan of water to a boil, then add the shrimp. Cook for 3 to 5 minutes, then transfer the shrimp to an ice bath to stop the cooking process and cool down the shrimp.

3. Add the shrimp to the bowl with the mayonnaise mixture and toss to coat. Fold in the scallions and roasted red peppers and season with pepper.

4. Line the hot dog buns with the lettuce, if desired, then spoon the shrimp mixture inside. Serve with potato chips and pickles on the side.

JERK-SPICED SHRIMP BURGER

I developed this recipe in an effort to wow an industry colleague. Kiano Moju is an LA-based culinary producer and food stylist of Kenyan descent who, through her company, Jikoni, has consulted and produced recipes and other content for some of the largest food media companies in the US. Kiano reached out to me on social media and asked me to contribute a recipe to her blog. I spent 2 days recipe testing this dish before sending the recipe over to her. She retested it and created a short video with a voiceover of me explaining the dish: juicy on the inside, crispy on the outside, and filled with a bunch of herbaceous flavors. It was a huge success!! I received tons of messages from her followers saying how much they enjoyed it, and it made me very happy to think that this burger is now going to be a feature at a lot of family BBQs and get-togethers to come.

SERVES: 4   PREP: 10 MIN   COOK: 15 MIN

1. Preheat the oven to 425°F.

2. In a food processor, place the shrimp, egg whites, scallions, panko, and jerk dry rub. Pulse to combine (there should be some chunks of shrimp). Shape the shrimp mixture into four ¾-inch-thick patties (see photo below).

3. In a large nonstick skillet over medium heat, melt the coconut oil. Add the patties and cook until golden brown and opaque throughout, 3 to 4 minutes per side. Remove from heat and squeeze lime juice all over the patties. Place the skillet in the oven and bake for 3 minutes.

4. Remove from the oven and assemble your burgers: spread the buns with tartar sauce, then top each one with lettuce, a shrimp patty, and sliced tomatoes. Serve and enjoy!

1 lb peeled and deveined large shrimp, chopped

2 egg whites

2 scallions, finely chopped

2 tbsp panko bread crumbs

1 tbsp Jerk Dry Rub (page 19)

1½ tbsp coconut oil

1 lime, halved

4 challah rolls or buns, split

¼ cup tartar sauce

2 cups shredded romaine lettuce, for serving

Beefsteak tomato, sliced, for serving

Poultry + Meat

JERK-MARINATED CHICKEN RASTA PASTA

Rasta Pasta was created by Lorraine Washington, a Jamaican chef who had a brief stint as a flight attendant. She was inspired by her travels to craft Jamaican "fusion" dishes that reflected her experiences—something that resonates with me a lot. The story behind this recipe goes that one day while working at her restaurant, Paradise Yard, in Negril, Jamaica, Chef Lorraine ran out of proteins during lunch service and had to improvise. She created a dish with ackee, house-made tomato sauce, and fettuccini. The construction workers who frequented the restaurant pointed out that the colors of the dish were reminiscent of the Rastafarian flag (red, gold, and green) and that the fettuccini resembled their dreadlocks—thus, Rasta Pasta was born. There have been hundreds of derivatives of this dish since its inception in the '80s. This is my version: an homage to Chef Lorraine to thank her for the inspiration.

SERVES: 8   PREP: 10 MIN + MARINATING   COOK: 30 MIN

1. In a large mixing bowl, toss the chicken thighs with the jerk marinade to coat, then allow to marinate at room temperature for 30 minutes.

2. Cook the fettuccini or spaghettini according to package instructions, then drain and set aside.

3. Heat a large frying pan over high heat and melt the coconut oil. Add the chicken thighs and cook for 5 minutes per side or until cooked through. Remove the thighs from the pan, then thinly slice them and set aside.

4. Meanwhile, make the coconut alfredo sauce: In a saucepan over medium-low heat, heat the coconut cream until lightly simmering. Add the garlic paste and Parmesan and whisk until emulsified.

5. In the pan used for frying the chicken, over high heat, sauté the julienned peppers for 3 minutes.

6. Stir the coconut alfredo sauce, as much as you desire, into the cooked pasta and mix well.

7. Serve immediately, topped with the sliced chicken and peppers.

6 boneless, skinless chicken thighs

¼ cup Jerk Marinade (page 19)

7 oz fettuccini or spaghettini

1 tbsp coconut oil

1 red bell pepper, julienned

1 yellow bell pepper, julienned

1 green bell pepper, julienned

COCONUT ALFREDO SAUCE

3 cups coconut cream

1 tbsp Garlic Paste (page 24)

¼ cup freshly grated Parmesan

MAPLE ADOBO CHICKEN

My introduction to Filipino cuisine was in the summer of 2018 in Pasadena, California. I was working on a film set as a catering/craft services chef for my girlfriend's uncle, Cecilio, who was the executive producer of the project. Cecilio and the cast of the show were predominantly Filipino, so during the course of filming, I was tasked with creating authentic Filipino offerings. This was huge—up until this point, my food had received rave reviews from production and talent alike, so I couldn't screw it up. I confided in Cecilio that I didn't know much about Filipino food (despite dating his niece, yikes!), and he reassured me that we would spend the next couple of days learning everything. We started off by visiting local Filipino grocers in the LA area, where I discovered some of the ingredients used, like tamarind, garlic, shrimp paste, and soy sauce. We then spent the next 2 days gorging ourselves on a variety of dishes from local restaurants, from beautiful briny pork sinigang broth to salty early-morning marinated tapas beef. Within 48 hours, I had been completely immersed in the food and culture.

I learned that adobo chicken is to the Filipino community what jerk chicken is to the Jamaican community, and if I wanted to impress, I'd have to master this dish! I spent the night learning how to make a classic adobo chicken dish, with Cecilio sharing all the tips and tricks his mother had passed on to him, which her mother had passed on to her. I think that when taking on another community's cuisine, it's important to have someone from that community explain the dish and method of preparation to ensure you do it justice. I've cooked multiple iterations of adobo chicken since that day, and I'm happy to say I've landed on a recipe that has won the stamp of approval from all the Titas and Lolas in my now-extended family.

SERVES: 8   PREP: 10 MIN   COOK: 1 HR 5 MIN

1 (5 to 6 lb) whole chicken, patted dry, giblets and neck removed

½ cup Pineapple Vinegar (page 27)

⅓ cup soy sauce

⅓ cup vegetable oil

4 tbsp maple syrup

4 cloves garlic, minced

½ tsp garlic powder

1 tsp freshly ground black pepper

2 tbsp unsalted butter

3 bay leaves

1. Preheat the oven to 425°F.

2. Spray a 12-inch cast-iron skillet with cooking spray, and place the chicken in the skillet.

3. In a medium saucepan, mix the pineapple vinegar, soy sauce, vegetable oil, maple syrup, garlic, garlic powder, and pepper and bring to a boil over high heat. Reduce the heat to medium, stir in the butter, and cook for 4 or 5 minutes, until thickened. (If you prefer a runnier sauce, simply melt the butter in the microwave and mix it in with the rest of the ingredients.) Transfer about a third of the mixture to a bowl and set aside.

4. Brush the remaining sauce all over the chicken, including under loose skin and inside the cavity. Place the bay leaves inside the chicken.

5. Bake for 30 minutes. Reduce the temperature to 350°F, brush the chicken on the top and sides with some of the reserved adobo sauce, and bake for 30 minutes more, or until the internal temperature reaches 165°F.

6. Remove from the oven, brush with the reserved sauce, and let rest for 10 minutes before slicing.

RUM-SOAKED CHICKEN

This is the dish I made when I was auditioning for Top Chef Canada. I wanted to use ingredients that represented me and that would really impress the judges. And guess what? It worked.

SERVES: 4   PREP: 10 MIN + MARINATING   COOK: 20 MIN

1. Make the rum marinade: In a food processor or blender, combine all the marinade ingredients and pulse until you reach a chunky consistency.

2. In a mixing bowl, combine the chicken with ⅓ cup rum marinade. Let marinate at room temperature for at least 20 minutes.

3. In a saucepan over medium heat, heat the remaining marinade gently to burn off the alcohol. Add the pineapple juice and continue to simmer until the liquid reduces by a third.

4. In a grill pan or skillet over medium-high heat, melt the coconut oil. Add the chicken and cook on each side until golden, 5 to 6 minutes per side. Once the chicken is cooked through, set aside and allow to rest for a few minutes.

5. Plate the chicken and spoon the pineapple juice sauce overtop, or allow your guests to dip their chicken in a bowl of sauce served on the table.

RUM MARINADE

1 bunch fresh thyme, leaves only
2 cups chopped fresh cilantro
¼ cup minced fresh ginger
⅓ cup Garlic Paste (page 24)
1 cup chopped scallions
1 bunch fresh basil
1 cup chopped white onions
1 cup olive oil
2 cups white rum

4 boneless, skin-on chicken quarters (legs and thighs)
1 cup pineapple juice
1 tbsp coconut oil

YASSA POULET

Preserving ancestral food and culture has always been one of the forces behind my drive for excellence in the culinary industry. And having positive role models to look up to and aspire to be like is an integral part of that development. I have never met Chef Pierre Thiam in person, but his drive, tenacity, passion, and resilience are all attributes of the kind of chef and person I aspire to be. Before I learned about him, I didn't have a deep understanding of the cuisine of the African continent, but now I view it as the culinary version of El Dorado. He bridged the gap between Africa and America, started his own sourcing company that provides jobs to farmers in need, and resurrected a centuries-old crop that had been forgotten—smuggling it in his luggage in order to serve it to guests at his restaurant in Harlem. That crop, fonio, is now available in grocery stores worldwide and is showing up on restaurant menus of chefs who are not even of African descent! My admiration for Thiam and what he has accomplished led to more research into West African ingredients, techniques, and recipes. This Senegalese spicy lemon chicken—or, as the locals would call it, yassa poulet—has become one of my favorite go-tos. I often serve it with fonio, which is definitely worth tracking down if you can.

SERVES: 6   PREP: 30 MIN + MARINATING   COOK: 1½ HR

2 tbsp Dijon mustard

½ cup lemon juice

2 tbsp Garlic Paste (page 24)

¼ cup canola or olive oil

1 whole chicken, cut into 8 pieces (or 6 chicken thighs)

4 cups julienned white onions

1 tbsp Herb Oil (page 26)

Salt and freshly ground black pepper

1 to 3 Pickled Scotch Bonnets (page 20)

1½ cups hot chicken stock

1 cup black or green olives, pitted and sliced

Chopped fresh flat-leaf parsley, for serving

Lemon or lime wedges, for serving

Cooked fluffy rice or fonio, for serving

1. In a small mixing bowl, combine the Dijon, lemon juice, garlic paste, and oil and whisk together.

2. Place the chicken pieces and onions in a large bowl and pour the marinade over top. Using your hands, rub the marinade into the chicken flesh. Cover with plastic wrap and let marinate in the fridge for a minimum of 3 hours (overnight is preferred).

3. Preheat the oven to 405°F.

4. In a 12-inch cast-iron skillet over high heat, heat the herb oil. Remove the chicken from the marinade and season with salt and pepper. Working in batches, brown the chicken in the skillet on both sides, about 5 minutes total per batch. Transfer to a wire rack placed over a baking sheet.

5. Add the marinated onions to the skillet and cook, stirring continuously. Reduce the heat to low and let the onions slowly caramelize, about 10 minutes. Use a spatula or wooden spoon to remove the onions.

6. Add the chicken pieces back to the skillet and pile the caramelized onions on top. Add the pickled Scotch bonnet and hot chicken stock. Bring the liquid to a simmer, then remove from heat and transfer the skillet to the oven to bake for 45 to 60 minutes, until the stock has reduced and the chicken skin is crispy.

7. Remove the skillet from the oven. Scatter with the sliced olives and some fresh herbs and lemon or lime wedges, if desired. Serve with fluffy rice or fonio.

COCONUT FRIED CHICKEN

This might sound very cliché coming from a Black chef, but I pride myself on great fried chicken. I spent a lot of time working toward not being pigeonholed for making food that often brings up negative connotations and stereotypes attached to our culture, but then I realized that there's nothing wrong with owning a specific talent or skill. I made a living off selling fried chicken for 5 years with my business The Dirty Bird Chicken + Waffles, franchised a whole restaurant concept, won multiple awards and accolades, and became a Food Network personality and judge because of this fried chicken. So why would I not embrace it and use the platform it's helped give me to let people know that our food culture is so much more?

I developed this coconut fried chicken recipe while on vacation in Jamaica. We had fresh coconuts, live chickens, and an abundance of herbs and spices. This is now my all-time favorite fried chicken recipe out of the 100,000 variations I've created over the last 10 years, so I hope you enjoy!

SERVES: 4   PREP: 10 MIN + MARINATING   COOK: 25 MIN

1. In a large bowl, toss together the chicken pieces, white pepper, salt, onion powder, garlic paste, and thyme to coat. Add the coconut cream and mix until the chicken is coated. Cover and refrigerate for 6 hours.

2. Make the seasoned flour: In a large shallow dish, combine the coconut flour, salt, white pepper, thyme, garlic powder, and onion powder.

3. Remove the chicken from the coconut cream and dredge each piece in the seasoned flour. Shake off any excess flour and transfer the chicken to a plate.

4. In a large Dutch oven or deep fryer, heat the coconut oil to 350°F. Add all the chicken to the pan or deep fryer and cook for 10 minutes. Turn the chicken pieces and cook for another 10 to 15 minutes, until cooked through.

5. Remove the chicken from the oil and transfer to a cooling rack set over a paper towel-lined baking sheet. Let sit for 10 minutes before serving. Finish with salt to taste.

1 whole chicken, cut into 8 pieces (or 4 chicken drumsticks and 4 thighs)

½ tsp white pepper

1 tbsp salt

¾ tsp onion powder

¼ tsp Garlic Paste (page 24)

¼ tsp ground thyme

2 cups coconut cream

SEASONED FLOUR

4 cups coconut flour

1 tbsp salt

½ tbsp white pepper

1 tsp ground thyme

1 tsp garlic powder

1 tsp onion powder

10 cups coconut oil, for frying

Salt, to taste

JERK-MARINATED CHICKEN COQ AU VIN

This dish holds a very special place in my heart. Part of my goal as a chef is to push Afro-Caribbean cuisine to the forefront, and this recipe has certainly helped me in doing that so far. I've received widespread acclaim for it from well-respected journalists and food critics who praise how creative and progressive it is, as well as how authentic it is to my Jamaican roots.

I created this dish when my close friend and fellow chef Shontelle Pinch moved to Jamaica, where she had purchased a beautiful 24-acre compound. Part of this compound was a farm where she keeps her own livestock and grows her own Scotch bonnet peppers. She then uses those Scotch bonnets to produce a hot sauce, Pinch, that is bottled and sold in grocery stores back in Toronto.

I went to visit her, and being back home in beautiful Jamaica, my native country, with access to the freshest ingredients, ignited a fire in my belly that I couldn't ignore. Within hours of arriving on the island, I had built an open fire with coconut shells and pimento wood as my fuel, gathered ingredients from the farm for my jerk marinade, and sourced a local Jamaican port wine for a French element I was inspired to add. Here is the result.

SERVES: 8   PREP: 20 MIN   COOK: 2 HR 15 MIN

1 whole chicken

½ cup Jerk Marinade (page 19)

2 tbsp coconut oil

1 cup small-diced shallots or whole pearl onions

2 carrots, cut into ½-inch cubes

1 cup sliced okra (sliced into ½- to ¾-inch-thick disks)

1 tbsp all-purpose flour

2½ cups red wine

2 cups chicken stock

4 tbsp unsalted butter

Mashed potatoes or rice pilaf, for serving

Pickled pearl onions, for serving (optional)

1. On a cutting board, place the chicken breast side down with legs toward you. Using sturdy scissors or poultry shears, cut along each side of the backbone to remove it, cutting through the rib bones as you go, to butterfly the chicken.

2. In a large bowl, combine the chicken and half the jerk marinade and massage the marinade into the chicken and under the skin.

3. Preheat your BBQ or smoker to high (350°F). Place the chicken skin side down on the grill over direct heat. Grill for 20 minutes, then, once the skin has some color, flip the chicken and continue to cook over indirect heat for an additional 60 minutes.

4. Remove the chicken from the BBQ or smoker and cut into eight pieces; cutting the chicken at the joints helps you get even-sized pieces.

5. Heat a cast-iron skillet or Dutch oven over medium-high heat and melt the coconut oil. Add the shallots, carrots, and okra and sweat until the shallots become translucent, about 5 minutes.

6. Add the flour and remaining jerk marinade and mix the ingredients well. Deglaze the pan with the red wine and chicken stock. Add the chicken pieces to the skillet and mix well. Reduce the heat to medium, cover with the lid and simmer on medium heat for 50 minutes.

8. Remove from heat, add the butter, and mix well. Serve over mashed potatoes or rice pilaf, garnished with a few pickled pearl onions if desired.

NOTE: *Shred and store any leftover chicken in the fridge, to use on the Tropical Jerk Stuffed-Crust Pizza on page 189.*

TROPICAL STUFFED-CRUST PIZZA

Once when I was working as a culinary consultant, a client asked me to come up with a dish that would appeal to various demographics based on their market research. They told me "tropical" flavors were on pace to be the food trend of the year, and they gave me the ultimate challenge: to create something with these flavors that multiple people with different food preferences and from different ethnic backgrounds would all enjoy. I had a bunch of different ideation sessions, did multiple tastings, and spent countless hours on recipe development, and still had nothing. Out of necessity (I was running out of time and funds!), I crafted this recipe after rummaging through my fridge. There I found some leftover Jerk-Marinated Chicken Coq au Vin (page 186), pineapple, frozen tomato sauce, and the last package of cheddar left over from my recipe testing. I was suddenly inspired! Choosing pizza as the vehicle, I was able to carefully incorporate the perfect amount of salty, sour, sweet, and spicy to create a harmonious balance of flavor. Tropical Stuffed-Crust Pizza was born!

MAKES: 1 PIZZA   **PREP: 15 MIN**   **COOK: 15 MIN**

1 recipe pizza dough (page 125)

Scotch Bonnet Oil (page 20), for drizzling

8 mozzarella cheese sticks

1 cup marinara sauce

2 cups shredded cheddar

1 cup shredded Jerk-Marinated Chicken Coq au Vin (page 186)

¼ cup diced pineapple

2 tbsp chopped scallions

¼ cup sliced red onions

Chopped scallions, for serving

1. Preheat the oven to 500°F.

2. On a lightly floured surface, roll out the pizza dough and place it on a pizza baking dish. Drizzle the dough with a bit of Scotch bonnet oil.

3. Lay the mozzarella sticks around the outer edge of the pizza dough. Bring the edge of the dough over the cheese, pressing to encase the cheese in dough.

4. Ladle the marinara sauce in the center of the dough and use the back of the ladle or a spatula to evenly distribute it across the dough.

5. Top with the cheddar, shredded jerk chicken, pineapple, scallions, and onions.

6. Bake for 10 to 15 minutes, or until the edge is golden brown. Serve hot, sprinkled with scallions.

NOTE: *If you love onions as much as I do, try adding them raw to the pizza once it is cooked instead, for an extra allium hit!*

STOUT GLAZED RIBS

In Jamaica we often cook with stout beer. So when I was working on the menu for my pop-up restaurant Yawd, I was inspired to do something with stout. It's bitter but creamy and has notes of chocolate, so why not pair it with ribs?

SERVES: 4   PREP: 10 MIN + MARINATING   COOK: 2 HR

2 lb pork ribs

STOUT MARINADE
12 oz Guinness stout
1 large onion, sliced
¼ cup soy sauce
¼ cup brown sugar
2 tbsp sesame oil
1 tbsp minced garlic

GLAZE
½ cup molasses
¼ cup soy sauce
1 tbsp chopped fresh flat-leaf
   parsley
1 tbsp minced garlic
¾ tsp freshly ground black
   pepper

1. Place the ribs in a large pan or resealable plastic bag.

2. Make the stout marinade: In a bowl, combine the marinade ingredients, then pour over the ribs. Cover the pan or seal the bag and marinate the ribs in the fridge for at least 8 hours.

3. Preheat the oven to 350°F.

4. Remove the ribs from the pan or plastic bag and wrap in a double layer of aluminum foil. Place on a baking sheet and bake for about 1½ hours.

5. Make the glaze: In a bowl, combine all the glaze ingredients, mixing well.

6. Remove the ribs from the oven, open the foil, and generously spread the ribs with half of the glaze. Return the ribs to the oven (unwrapped and still on the baking sheet) and bake for an additional 30 minutes.

7. Remove from the oven and allow the ribs to rest for 15 minutes before serving. Drizzle with the remaining glaze.

BROWN STEW PORK CHOPS

Brown stew pork is a popular Jamaican dish that uses pork leg or shoulder. I love the stew flavor, but I wanted to elevate it by combining it with a sauce africaine, and instead of using braised pork, I tried pork chops. They're delicious with Coconut Milk Mash (page 105), Okra Pilaf (page 109) or Cassava au Gratin (page 102) served alongside.

SERVES: 4   PREP: 5 MIN   COOK: 30 MIN

1. Prepare the pork chops: In a mixing bowl, combine the coconut oil, brown sugar, jerk dry rub, and garlic paste. Rub onto the pork chops.

2. In a cast-iron skillet over high heat, sear the pork chops for 5 minutes per side, or until tender and the pork is cooked (with an internal temperature of 145°F). Transfer to a baking sheet.

3. Make the sauce africaine: Add the onions and bell peppers to the skillet and cook on high heat until the onions are translucent, about 5 minutes. Add the tomatoes and mix well. Deglaze the pan with the beef stock.

4. Add the demi-glace and thyme, and as the mixture comes to a simmer, stir with a wooden spoon to remove any sediment from the bottom of the skillet.

5. Fold in the basil leaves and coconut cream, then add the pork chops and their juices back to the skillet. Smother the pork chops with the sauce. Remove from heat and serve, sprinkled with parsley.

PORK CHOPS

1 tbsp coconut oil

1 tbsp light brown sugar

1 tbsp Jerk Dry Rub (page 19)

1 tbsp Garlic Paste (page 24)

4 bone-in pork chops

SAUCE AFRICAINE

1 large yellow onion, julienned

1 red bell pepper, julienned

1 plum tomato, medium-diced

1 cup beef stock

½ cup store-bought demi-glace gravy mix

1 sprig thyme, stem removed

6 fresh basil leaves, cut into chiffonade

¼ cup coconut cream

Chopped fresh flat-leaf parsley, for serving

CARIBBEAN-SPICED STUFFED MEATBALLS

I was working a consultant job for a large hospitality group, making several dishes at the same time, including stuffed meatballs. I had all these different ingredients on the counter and accidentally knocked my jerk spice mix into my meatball mix. It was too late to go back, so I just went with it! As it turns out, it was a happy accident that totally worked. The cheese at the center cools down the spice, and the glaze adds the perfect amount of sweetness.

SERVES: 6   PREP: 15 MIN   COOK: 25 MIN

STUFFED MEATBALLS

9 oz mozzarella

1 lb ground beef or lamb

1 cup bread crumbs

1 egg

1 tbsp Jerk Dry Rub (page 19)

3 tbsp Garlic Paste (page 24)

Salt and freshly ground black pepper

1 tbsp coconut oil

TOMATO PAN SAUCE

½ cup tomato paste

1 tbsp Garlic Paste (page 24)

1 (28 oz) can crushed tomatoes

1 (14½ oz) can diced tomatoes with juice

1 tsp brown sugar (optional)

Cooked white rice, for serving

Fresh herbs, chopped, for serving

1. Make the stuffed meatballs: Cut the mozzarella into 1-inch cubes and set aside.

2. In a medium bowl, combine the ground beef or lamb, bread crumbs, egg, jerk dry rub, and garlic paste. Season with salt and pepper and stir to combine.

3. Scoop up 2 tbsp of the meatball mixture and, using your hands, start to shape it into a ball. Press one cube of mozzarella into the center of the ball, sealing the meat tightly around the cheese. Repeat with the remaining meatball mixture and cheese.

4. In a large skillet over medium-high heat, melt the coconut oil. Add the meatballs and brown on all sides, about 3 minutes. When the meatballs have developed a nice crust, remove them from the skillet and wipe the skillet clean.

5. Make the tomato pan sauce: Return the skillet to the stovetop over medium heat. Add the tomato paste and garlic paste and cook, stirring occasionally to prevent scorching, for 3 to 4 minutes. Stir in the crushed tomatoes, diced tomatoes, and sugar (if using). Reduce the heat to medium-low and simmer, uncovered, until the flavors have blended, about 10 minutes.

6. Return the meatballs to the skillet and spoon the sauce over them. Cover and simmer for about 8 minutes, or until the meatballs are cooked through.

7. Serve with white rice, garnished with chopped fresh herbs.

CURRY GOAT SHEPHERD'S PIE

When someone passes away in Jamaica, it's not enough to celebrate their life for one day or even a week. Instead, we honor them with what we call a nine night, where friends and family gather for nine consecutive days. With everyone over, you know there's going to be a lot of good food going down. One of the dishes always served is a goat soup and the other a curry goat.

It was my girlfriend who suggested this recipe combination. The filling for it is exactly as it would be if I was making curry goat, and the topping is exactly as if I was making a traditional shepherd's pie. For a guy who loves both, it's a win-win.

SERVES: 6   PREP: 20 MIN   COOK: 1 HR

1. Make the meat filling: Add the coconut oil to a large skillet and place it over medium-high heat for 2 minutes. Add the onions and cook for 5 minutes, stirring occasionally.

2. Add the ground goat or lamb to the skillet and break it apart with a wooden spoon.

3. Add the curry paste, garlic paste, fennel seeds, thyme, and celery. Cook, stirring often, for 6 to 8 minutes, or until the meat is browned.

4. Meanwhile, boil the potatoes: Place the potatoes in a large pot and cover them with water. Bring to a boil, then reduce the heat to a simmer and cook until the potatoes are fork-tender, 10 to 15 minutes.

5. To the pot with the meat filling, add the tomato purée, tomato paste, and flour. Stir until well incorporated and no clumps of tomato paste remain. Add the beef stock, frozen peas and carrots, and frozen corn. Bring the liquid to a boil, then reduce to a simmer. Simmer for 5 minutes, stirring occasionally.

6. Transfer the meat mixture to a casserole dish, about 7 × 9 inches, and set aside. Preheat the oven to 400°F.

7. Drain the potatoes in a colander. Return the potatoes to their hot pot and let them rest for 1 minute to evaporate any remaining liquid.

8. Make the potato topping: To the potatoes, add the butter, coconut milk, garlic powder, salt, and pepper. Mash the potatoes and stir until all the ingredients are mixed together. Add most of the Parmesan and stir until well combined.

9. Spoon the mashed potatoes on top of the meat in the casserole dish (photo 1). Carefully spread into an even layer, and sprinkle with the remaining Parmesan (photo 2). If the baking dish looks very full, place it on a rimmed baking sheet so that the filling doesn't bubble over into your oven.

10. Bake, uncovered, for 25 to 30 minutes. Allow to cool for 15 minutes before serving. Garnish with chopped parsley.

MEAT FILLING

2 tbsp coconut oil

1 onion, small-diced

1 lb ground goat or lamb

2 tbsp Curry Paste (page 21)

3 tbsp Garlic Paste (page 24)

1 tbsp fennel seeds

1 tsp dried thyme

1 stalk celery, small-diced

½ cup canned tomato purée

3 tbsp tomato paste

2 tbsp all-purpose flour

1 cup beef stock

1 cup frozen mixed peas and carrots

½ cup frozen corn kernels

POTATO TOPPING

1½ to 2 lb russet potatoes (about 2 large potatoes), peeled and cut into 1-inch cubes

½ cup unsalted butter

1 cup full-fat coconut milk

½ tsp garlic powder

½ tsp salt

¼ tsp freshly ground black pepper

¼ cup freshly grated Parmesan

Chopped fresh flat-leaf parsley or scallions, for serving

COFFEE-CRUSTED STEAK

Everyone knows about the famous Jamaican Blue Mountain coffee: it's hard to find, and expensive when you do, but it's delicious. I came back to Canada from Jamaica once with some of this coffee in my suitcase, and I used it in everything. One day I tried it in a spice rub on steak, and I never looked back.

SERVES: 4   PREP: 2 MIN + CHILLING   COOK: 6 MIN

COFFEE SPICE RUB
2 tbsp ancho chili powder
2 tbsp ground coffee beans
1 tbsp brown sugar
1 tbsp smoked paprika
1 tsp dried oregano
1 tsp ground coriander
1 tsp garlic powder
1 tsp crushed red pepper flakes

2 (16 oz) ribeye steaks
2 tbsp coconut oil

1. Make the coffee spice rub: In a mixing bowl, combine the ancho chili powder, ground coffee, brown sugar, smoked paprika, oregano, coriander, garlic powder, and pepper flakes. Whisk the spices together until well combined.

2. Pat the steaks dry, ensuring they are bone-dry. Then apply 2 tbsp of spice rub to each side of the steaks.

3. Place the steaks on a wire rack set inside a rimmed baking sheet and chill, uncovered, in the fridge for 1 hour.

4. In a large skillet over medium-high heat, melt the coconut oil. Add the steaks to the skillet and cook for 3 minutes on each side for medium-rare.

5. Place the cooked steaks on a clean wire rack and let rest for 5 minutes before slicing. Cut the steaks into ½-inch-thick slices and serve with Coconut Milk Mash (page 105) Trinidadian Corn Pie (page 115), Okra Pilaf (page 109), or OG Potato Salad (page 89).

OXTAIL GNOCCHI

When I was on Top Chef Canada, I was eliminated on a pasta challenge. After I was sent home, I made it my mission to perfect my pasta skills. At Yawd we originally thought of regular gnocchi for the menu, but then my sous-chef, Alex Fields, had the idea for us to use cassava instead of potatoes (and spent the next 14 days solely making cassava gnocchi!). Naturally, I wanted to give my twist to it, so I decided to add oxtail. Oxtail and dumplings is a very traditional Jamaican dish, so this was a progressive spin on the classic. And just like that, a signature dish was born.

SERVES: 6   PREP: 10 MIN + MARINATING   COOK: 8 HR

1. Make the oxtail ragu: In a large mixing bowl, combine the oxtail, onions, scallions, garlic paste, thyme, paprika, soy sauce, and Worcestershire sauce. Cover and marinate for at least 4 hours, or overnight, in the fridge, stirring occasionally.

2. Remove the oxtail from the marinade and gently shake off any excess marinade back into the bowl. Set the marinade aside.

3. In a large cast-iron skillet over medium-high heat, melt the coconut oil. When the oil is hot, not burning, place the oxtail in the pot and brown on all sides. Remove the browned oxtail and transfer to a slow cooker. Deglaze the skillet with water and pour that liquid over the oxtail.

4. Add enough water to the slow cooker to cover the oxtail. Also toss in the marinade, tomatoes, carrots, and beef bouillon powder. Set on high and cook for about 7 hours, until the meat becomes tender and falls off the bone.

5. When ready, remove the oxtail from the slow cooker and let it cool (leaving the ragu in the slow cooker). Remove the meat from the bones (and reserve the bones to make stock at a later time). Add the pulled oxtail meat back to the slow cooker, then add the lima beans, tomato paste, and more water, if needed.

6. Simmer, uncovered, for 1 hour, skimming the fat off the top and stirring occasionally. In the last 30 minutes of cooking time, add the port wine and the jerk marinade.

OXTAIL RAGU

5 lb oxtail, trimmed

2 cups chopped white onions

1½ cups chopped scallions

1 tbsp Garlic Paste (page 24)

1 bunch fresh thyme, stems removed

1 tbsp smoked paprika

1 tbsp soy sauce

1 tbsp Worcestershire sauce

1 tbsp coconut oil

1 cup chopped tomatoes

2 cups cubed carrots

½ cup beef bouillon powder

2 cups canned lima beans, rinsed and drained

2 tbsp tomato paste

1 cup port wine

2 tbsp Jerk Marinade (page 19)

CONTINUED

CASSAVA GNOCCHI

1 lb cassava, peeled and cubed

1 cup all-purpose flour

1 tsp salt

1 egg

Freshly grated Parmesan, for
    serving (optional)

7. Meanwhile, make the cassava gnocchi: Place the cassava in a large pot and cover it with water. Bring to a boil and cook until fork-tender, about 20 minutes, then remove from the pot and let cool. Pass the cooled cassava through a potato ricer (alternatively, you can mash it with a fork or potato masher).

8. On a flat surface, mix together the flour and salt. Make a well in the middle and add the egg and cassava to the well (photo 1). Mix everything together with your fingers to form a soft dough (photo 2); it should not stick to your fingers.

9. On a lightly floured surface, cut out small amounts of the dough and roll them out to form ropes, then cut the ropes into ¾-inch pieces (photo 3). Slide each piece across the tines of a fork, squeezing a little (but not too hard), just to make marks (photo 4). Repeat until all the dough is used up.

10. Sprinkle the gnocchi with a bit of flour and toss them gently so they don't stick together. Let the gnocchi rest for 20 minutes before cooking.

11. Bring a large pot of salted water to a boil and cook the gnocchi for about 4 minutes; you know they are ready when they float to the top.

12. In a large frying pan, combine the pulled oxtail ragu with the cooked gnocchi. Heat for 30 seconds over high heat, gently tossing, to combine and warm through.

13. Serve immediately, topped with freshly grated Parmesan if desired. Enjoy!

NOTE: *Keep any leftover ragu from this recipe to use in the nachos on page 74.*

Desserts

TOASTED COCONUT CHEESECAKE

Coconut is my favorite ingredient to work with. The first time I made this dessert, it was for a client who was obsessed with coconut cheesecake. I went into the kitchen and threw some stuff together, and this awesome cake was born.

SERVES: 8   PREP: 20 MIN + RESTING AND CHILLING   COOK: 1 HR 20 MIN

1. Preheat the oven to 375°F. Lightly grease or line with parchment paper a 9-inch springform pan.

2. Make the coconut crust: In a small bowl, combine the graham cracker crumbs, toasted coconut, sugar, and melted coconut oil. Press the crumb mixture into the bottom of the prepared pan.

3. Wrap the outside of the springform pan with a double or triple layer of aluminum foil. (This serves two separate functions: first, the foil will act as a buffer between the direct heat of the oven and the pan so that the cheesecake bakes more evenly; second, it will catch any excess oil from the crust that may leak out while baking and hit the bottom of your oven.)

4. Make the coconut custard: In a medium saucepan, combine the coconut cream, vanilla, sugar, and cream cheese and bring to a light simmer. Using a whisk, mix well until the mixture is a smooth consistency, free of lumps.

5. Continuing to whisk, add the eggs, one at a time, until fully incorporated. Add the coconut extract, if using. Using your thermometer probe, check the temperature of your custard. It is ready when it has reached 167°F.

6. Pour the coconut custard over the prepared coconut crust base and bake for 40 minutes. After 40 minutes, turn off the oven and allow the cheesecake to remain inside for another 40 minutes; this helps "steam" the cheesecake and firm up the soft and runny middle for a more Japanese-style cheesecake texture. Remove from the oven and allow to cool at room temperature.

7. Once cooled, chill the cheesecake in the fridge for about 2 hours (do not put the cheesecake in the fridge if it is still warm or it will crack).

8. Serve chilled with berries or tropical fruits, coconut caramel sauce, and coconut flakes, as desired.

COCONUT CRUST

1⅓ cups graham cracker crumbs

¼ cup unsweetened shredded coconut, toasted

¼ cup granulated sugar

⅓ cup melted coconut oil

COCONUT CUSTARD

2 cups coconut cream

1 tsp vanilla extract

1 cup granulated sugar

3 (8 oz) packages cream cheese

3 eggs

1 tsp coconut extract (optional)

TOPPINGS (OPTIONAL)

Berries or tropical fruits

Coconut Caramel Sauce (page 216)

Coconut flakes

COCONUT MILK FRENCH TOAST WITH PINEAPPLE FLAMBÉ

This dish was inspired by my time on Turks: being on an island, cooking with fresh ingredients, and trying to do something different and fun. Here I use a Caribbean bread called hard dough, which is perfect for French toast, but you can use regular sliced bread instead.

SERVES: 4   PREP: 10 MIN   COOK: 30 MIN

COCONUT MILK FRENCH TOAST

4 eggs

½ cup full-fat coconut milk

1 tsp vanilla extract

2 tsp granulated sugar

½ tsp ground cinnamon

Pinch of salt

⅓ cup coconut oil or unsalted butter, for frying

8 thick slices hard dough bread (see recipe introduction)

8 pineapple rings (use the top half of the pineapple used below)

PINEAPPLE FLAMBÉ

8 pineapple rings (use the top half of the pineapple used below)

2 tbsp coconut oil or unsalted butter

½ large pineapple, peeled and cubed (about 2 cups)

⅓ cup granulated sugar

¼ cup spiced or dark rum

1 tsp ground cinnamon

Coconut flakes, for serving

1. Make the coconut milk French toast: In a bowl, whisk together the eggs, coconut milk, vanilla, sugar, cinnamon, and salt.

2. In a frying pan over medium heat, melt the coconut oil or butter (or half of each).

3. Dip each side of a bread slice in the egg mixture, giving each side a few seconds in the mixture. Press a pineapple ring firmly into one side of each slice of bread.

4. Working in batches, transfer the soaked bread to the hot pan, pineapple ring-side down. Cook for 2 to 3 minutes, until golden brown, then flip and cook for another 2 to 3 minutes on the other side. Repeat until all the bread slices are cooked. Keep warm in the oven.

5. Make the pineapple flambé: In a large sauté pan over medium-high heat, melt the coconut oil or butter. Coat each side of the pineapple cubes in sugar and immediately place them in the hot oil.

6. Cook the pineapple until it is starting to caramelize on one side, about 5 minutes. Carefully flip the pineapple cubes over and continue to cook for another 4 to 5 minutes, until the pineapple is softened and caramelized. Juice should release from the pineapple and mix with the caramel to form a lovely golden caramel sauce.

7. Add the rum to flambé the pineapple, removing the pan from the heat if the flame becomes daunting (and adding a splash of pineapple juice to calm it if needed). Sprinkle with cinnamon.

8. Serve the toast warm, with the pineapple flambé and a sprinkling of coconut flakes.

BROWN SUGAR & TAMARIND CINNAMON ROLLS

I've never prided myself on being an amazing baker—I would say I possess just-above-average baking skills. To be honest, it requires too much structure for me; you need precision, patience, and a whole lot of finesse. What I love about cooking is the freedom to make decisions on a whim and changes during the process. And you also get to eat your mistakes, whereas baking is very unforgiving in that department!

But I've been a lover of cinnamon rolls for as long as I can remember. To pay my way through culinary school, I moonlighted as a customer service agent at a call center. There was a well-known chain specializing in cinnamon rolls that I would often indulge in after my shift—as a reward to myself for waking up at 5 a.m., completing a full day's worth of classes, and then working from 4 p.m. to midnight. This was my routine for 18 months straight. When I was fresh out of culinary school and working as a broke line cook, I could no longer afford to purchase the rolls, so I took a shot at making them myself. I added tamarind because I didn't have enough money to buy butter (and I had tamarind paste in my pantry from experimenting with some jerk-style chicken pad thai the week before). Who knew it would actually taste good? Cinnamon rolls will always be symbolic for me as a reward for hard work.

MAKES: 9 ROLLS   PREP: 15 MIN + RISING   COOK: 25 MIN

1. Make the dough: Warm the milk to around 110°F (I do this by microwaving it in a microwave-safe bowl for 40 to 45 seconds). Transfer the warm milk to the bowl of a stand mixer fitted with the paddle attachment and sprinkle the yeast on top.

2. Add the sugar, egg, egg yolk, and melted butter. Mix until well combined. Stir in the bread flour and salt until a dough begins to form.

3. Using the dough hook attachment, knead the dough on medium speed for 8 minutes. If it's too sticky (meaning it's sticking to the bottom of the bowl), add in 2 tbsp more bread flour. Alternatively, you can use your hands to knead the dough for 8 to 10 minutes on a well-floured surface.

4. Transfer the dough ball to a well-oiled bowl and cover with plastic wrap and a warm towel. Allow the dough to rise on the kitchen counter for 1 to 1½ hours, or until doubled in size.

5. Make the filling: In a small bowl, whisk together the brown sugar and cinnamon. Add the butter and then the tamarind pulp and continue to mix until a paste forms.

DOUGH

¾ cup milk (whole or 2% preferred)

2¼ tsp instant or active dry yeast (¼ oz package yeast)

¼ cup granulated sugar

1 egg plus 1 egg yolk, room temperature

¼ cup unsalted butter, melted

3 cups bread flour, plus more for dusting

¾ tsp salt

FILLING

⅔ cup dark brown sugar (light brown also works)

1½ tbsp ground cinnamon

¼ cup unsalted butter, softened

¼ cup tamarind pulp

CONTINUED

CREAM CHEESE FROSTING

4 oz cream cheese, softened

3 tbsp unsalted butter, softened

¾ cup icing sugar

½ tsp vanilla extract

6. After the dough has doubled in size, transfer it to a well-floured surface and roll out into a 9 × 14-inch rectangle (photo 1).

7. Using a spoon or an offset spatula, smear the filling all over the dough (photo 2). Tightly roll up the dough, starting from the 9-inch side and ending seam side down, making sure to seal the edges of the dough as best you can. You will probably need to trim off about an inch from both ends of the dough, as the ends won't be as full of cinnamon sugar as we want them to be!

8. Using a serrated knife, cut the roll nine even pieces (photo 3). Grease and line a 9-inch square baking pan or a 9-inch round cake pan with parchment paper. Transfer the dough sections to the pan, cut side up.

9. Cover with plastic wrap and a warm towel and let rise again on the kitchen counter for 30 to 45 minutes.

10. Preheat the oven to 350°F.

11. Remove the towel and plastic wrap from the pan. Bake the cinnamon rolls for 20 to 25 minutes, or until they are just slightly golden brown on the edges; you want to underbake them a little so they stay soft in the middle. Remove from the oven and allow to cool for 5 to 10 minutes before frosting.

12. Make the cream cheese frosting: In the bowl of a stand mixer fitted with the whisk attachment, combine the cream cheese, butter, icing sugar, and vanilla. Beat until smooth and fluffy. Spread over the cinnamon rolls and serve immediately. Enjoy!

PLANTAIN BEIGNETS

In parts of Africa, specifically Nigeria, Sierra Leone, and sometimes Ghana, there is a sweet, fried round donut tossed in icing sugar called a puff puff. In France, and in New Orleans, a similar donut is called a beignet. I wanted to make my own Afro-Caribbean version of this treat, which is why I went with a plantain dough, like they do in Africa, and added a plantain custard. This is a recipe I am truly proud of and happy to call my signature dessert.

MAKES: 15 TO 18 BEIGNETS   **PREP: 10 MIN + CHILLING**   **COOK: 30 MIN**

1. Make the plantain purée: In a saucepan of boiling water, blanch the plantains for 3 to 5 minutes, until soft. Remove from the water and mash to create a purée. Set aside 1 cup of the plantain purée for the custard.

2. Make the plantain dough: In a large bowl, combine the remaining plantain purée with the warm cream and yeast, and stir to dissolve the yeast. Add the sugar and egg whites and blend well. Mix in the flour and beat until smooth. Cover the bowl and chill in the fridge for at least 3 hours and up to 24 hours.

3. When ready, remove the dough from the fridge and let it come to room temperature before frying. This takes about 20 minutes.

4. Make the plantain custard: In a blender, combine the 1 cup reserved plaintain purée, sugar, vanilla, and egg yolks. Pulse until the ingredients have combined, then slowly incorporate the melted butter until the mixture has emulsified. Keep warm.

5. Line a baking sheet with paper towel. In a saucepan over medium-low heat, heat the oil until it reaches 360°F. Use a spoon or ice-cream scoop to scoop up portions of the dough (you're aiming for 18 in total) and, working in batches of 4, add to the oil. Fry the beignets until golden brown, about 8 to 10 minutes. If the beignets do not pop up (which shows they are ready), the oil is not hot enough. Place the beignets on the paper towel to soak up any excess oil. Repeat until all the dough is used up.

6. Transfer the warm plantain custard to a piping bag fitted with a tip. Carefully fill the beignets with custard.

7. Shake icing sugar on top of the hot beignets, and serve warm.

PLANTAIN PURÉE

2 ripe plantains

PLANTAIN DOUGH

½ cup heavy or whipping cream, warmed

1 tbsp instant yeast

¼ cup granulated sugar

2 cups egg whites (about 8 to 10 eggs)

2 cups all-purpose flour

PLANTAIN CUSTARD

½ cup granulated sugar

1 tsp vanilla extract

4 egg yolks

3 cups warm melted unsalted butter

4 cups vegetable oil, for frying

Icing sugar, for dusting

STICKY GINGER PUDDING

This is a play on Jamaican sweet potato pudding—a pudding that is baked in a cast-iron Dutch oven lined with banana leaves and covered with a lid, which is then placed in a bed of hot amber charcoals and covered with more charcoals using a shovel. What you get is a pudding with a crispy top and bottom and a soft, gooey center. This recipe always reminds me of Christmas, because my grandmother would build a charcoal fire pit in our backyard and make a bunch of these puddings to fill orders from our neighbors.

SERVES: 10   PREP: 20 MIN   COOK: 50 MIN

2 tbsp unsalted butter

1 tbsp all-purpose flour, for dusting

BATTER

20 dates, pitted

1 tsp baking soda

½ cup salted butter, melted

½ cup brown sugar

¼ cup maple syrup

½ cup minced fresh ginger

3 large eggs

2 cups all-purpose flour

2 tsp baking powder

2 tbsp ground ginger

½ tsp salt

1 cup Jamaican ginger beer

COCONUT CARAMEL SAUCE

1 cup unsalted butter

1 cup brown sugar

½ cup maple syrup

1 cup coconut cream

Vanilla ice cream or Rum & Raisin Ice Cream (page 220), for serving

1. Preheat the oven to 350°F. Grease a cast-iron skillet or 8-inch square baking pan very well with the 2 tbsp butter (butter your fingers and rub it all down, making sure to get in all the crevices). Sprinkle with 1 tbsp or so of flour, tilting the pan and shaking it over the sink until the entire inside of the pan is coated with flour. Set aside.

2. Make the batter: In a small bowl, combine the dates with 2 cups boiling water and the baking soda and allow to soften, about 8 minutes.

3. Meanwhile, in the bowl of a stand mixer fitted with the paddle attachment, combine the melted butter, brown sugar, maple syrup, and minced ginger. Mix in the eggs, one at a time.

4. In a large bowl, sift together the flour, baking powder, ground ginger, and salt.

5. Strain the softened dates and add to a blender along with the Jamaican ginger beer, and pulse until a smooth paste forms.

6. Using a plastic spatula, fold the date mixture into your egg and butter mixture and mix well. Slowly add the flour mixture, mixing until fully incorporated.

7. Pour the batter into the prepared pan. Bake for 30 to 35 minutes, until the top is firm and a toothpick inserted in the center comes out clean. Remove from the oven and let rest in the pan.

8. While the cake is resting, make the coconut caramel sauce: In a saucepan over medium-low heat, melt the butter with the brown sugar, maple syrup, and coconut cream. Stir occasionally until bubbles appear in the center. Reduce the heat to low and continue cooking at a low simmer for about 15 minutes, until the sauce has thickened and coats the back of a spoon. Remove from heat and set aside to cool and continue to thicken.

9. Carefully invert the cake out of the pan and onto a plate. Using a toothpick, poke numerous holes in the top of the cake. Pour some of the sauce over the cake and allow the cake to absorb it. Pour a little more over the cake and let it absorb again. Repeat until the cake has absorbed all the sauce and becomes moist and dense.

10. Serve the sticky ginger pudding at room temperature or slightly warmed, with vanilla or rum & raisin ice cream!

COCONUT & GINGER BUDINO

My Jamaican chef friend Noel Cunningham made this for me. He's one of those rare talents who is skilled in both cooking and baking. He got me into desserts and inspired me to up my game. A traditional budino is an Italian custard similar to a panna cotta but a little on the creamier side, as it is thickened using starch and not gelatin. Once I received the base recipe from Chef Noel, I swapped out some of the whipping cream for coconut milk and added some ginger for an Afro-Caribbean twist.

SERVES: 6   PREP: 10 MIN + CHILLING   COOK: 20 MIN

1. Make the budino: In a medium bowl, whisk the egg yolks with 2 tbsp coconut milk, 2 tbsp cream, the ginger juice, and the cornstarch. Set aside.

2. In a medium saucepan over medium heat, heat the remaining coconut milk and cream with the sea salt for 3 to 5 minutes, until the salt is fully dissolved. Remove from heat.

3. In a separate saucepan over medium heat, heat the sugar until dissolved, stirring with a wooden spoon until it turns dark brown.

4. Pour the sugar into the warm cream mixture. Whisk in the yolk mixture, a little at a time, until fluffy. Cook on low heat for about 6 minutes, until the mixture thickens.

5. Pour the mixture into six ramekins or small bowls and cover each with plastic wrap. Chill in the fridge for at least 30 minutes.

6. While the budino is chilling, make the salted caramel sauce: In a saucepan over medium heat, melt the butter and brown sugar for about 6 minutes, until they turn an amber color. Add the whipping cream and salt and bring to a simmer, whisking continuously to ensure the mixture is smooth and lump-free, just 1 or 2 minutes.

7. Remove the budino from the fridge and unwrap. Pour the warm salted caramel sauce over the top of each bowl and serve.

BUDINO

4 egg yolks

1½ cups full-fat coconut milk

1½ cups heavy or whipping cream

2 tbsp juiced ginger (fresh ginger processed in a juicer)

¼ cup cornstarch

1 tsp sea salt

1 cup granulated sugar

SALTED CARAMEL SAUCE

8 tbsp unsalted butter

1 cup brown sugar

¾ cup heavy or whipping cream

1½ tsp salt

RUM & RAISIN ICE CREAM

This traditional Jamaican ice-cream flavor always reminds me of home. On the occasional Sunday (as a rare treat), after an early dinner, my family would shower, get into our Sunday best, and head over to Devon House, an old Jamaican mansion where ice-cream vendors would gather. We would all get to pick our favorite flavor and then run around the property. You can probably guess which flavor I chose.

SERVES: 8   PREP: 20 MIN + SOAKING AND FREEZING   COOK: 5 MIN

⅔ cup raisins

⅓ cup spiced rum

2 tbsp vanilla extract

2 cups heavy or whipping cream

⅔ cup sweetened condensed milk, room temperature

1 tsp ground cinnamon

1. Fully chill a 4½ × 8½-inch loaf pan in the freezer.

2. In a saucepan over medium heat, combine the raisins, rum, and 1 tbsp vanilla. Bring to a light simmer, then turn off the heat and leave uncovered for 30 to 60 minutes to allow the raisins to soak up the rum and soften.

3. In the bowl of a stand mixer fitted with the whisk attachment, whip the cream and remaining vanilla on high for 3 to 4 minutes, or until the cream solidifies and forms stiff peaks. Be careful not to overmix.

4. Using a spatula, gradually fold the condensed milk into the whipped cream; add just a little at a time to prevent the cream from deflating. Next, again adding a little at a time, fold the raisin and rum mixture into the cream. Add the cinnamon and fold until incorporated.

5. Pour the mixture into the chilled loaf pan, using the back of a spoon to distribute it evenly around the pan. Cover with plastic wrap. Freeze for at least 6 hours or overnight for best results.

6. When ready, let the ice cream soften for 10 to 15 minutes at room temperature before serving.

JAMAICAN ICE-CREAM CAKE SANDWICHES

These are ice-cream sandwiches, but served with bulla cake, a dense ginger cake that reminds me of my childhood. As teenagers, my friends and I would use a stack of milk crates to block off the street we lived on so we could play cricket. The winners of the cricket match would be rewarded by the losers, and bulla cake was often the post-match snack of choice. I decided to pair it here with an avocado ice cream because bulla cake is traditionally served with ripe avocados—when it isn't being eaten as an ice-cream sandwich.

SERVES: 6   PREP: 15 MIN + FREEZING   COOK: 30 MIN

1. Fully chill a 4½ × 8½-inch loaf pan in the freezer.

2. Make the avocado ice cream: Scoop the solid parts of the canned coconut milk into a high-speed blender and add the avocados, frozen banana chunks, maple syrup, lemon juice, and vanilla. Blend until smooth and creamy.

3. Pour the mixture into the chilled loaf pan and use the back of a spoon to distribute it evenly around the pan. Freeze for at least 4 hours or overnight for best results.

4. Preheat the oven to 350°F and line two baking sheets with parchment paper.

5. Make the bulla cakes: In a saucepan over low heat, combine ¾ cup water with the butter, vanilla, brown sugar, ginger, and salt. Stir for 5 minutes, until the sugar dissolves and the butter melts. Remove from heat and set aside to cool.

6. Into a mixing bowl, sift the flour, baking powder, baking soda, and cinnamon. Slowly pour the sugar mixture into the bowl, stirring to bring everything together.

7. Turn the dough out onto a lightly floured work surface and knead for 5 minutes, or until smooth and elastic. Roll the dough out to 1 inch thick. Using a 4-inch cookie cutter, cut the dough into 12 rounds.

8. Transfer the rounds to the prepared baking sheets. Bake for 25 minutes, or until cooked through and golden brown. Remove from the oven and allow to cool completely.

9. Once the bulla cakes have fully cooled, assemble the sandwiches: Place one bulla cake top side down on a plate, then scoop two scoops of avocado ice cream on top. Add the second bulla cake and gently press down to create a big ice-cream cake sandwich. Repeat with the remaining cakes and ice cream.

AVOCADO ICE CREAM

1½ cups full-fat coconut milk, refrigerated overnight

2 ripe avocados, peeled, halved, and pitted

1 ripe banana, cut into chunks and frozen

3 tbsp maple syrup

2 tbsp lemon juice

1 tsp vanilla extract

BULLA CAKES

2 tbsp unsalted butter

1 tbsp vanilla extract

1½ cups firmly packed brown sugar

2 tsp minced fresh ginger

2 tsp salt

4 cups all-purpose flour

1 tbsp baking powder

2 tsp baking soda

½ tsp ground cinnamon

Acknowledgments

This book came to fruition through a series of events that took place in perfect succession. I want to thank Michelle Arbus for seeing my potential and going to bat for me without us ever having met. Thanks to you, my dream of being a cookbook author is now a reality. I also want to thank my editor, Lindsay Paterson, for being kind, exceptionally patient, and my number one source of motivation. When I felt like I had nothing else left to give or hit a wall creatively, you would always find a way to put the batteries in my back to get me back on track. Thank you to my friend Joanna Fox, who also happens to be an amazing writer. You did a tremendous job of helping me navigate through this foreign space. Without you, I certainly wouldn't have been able to find my voice on the page and tell my story how I intended. I also want to thank my talent managers, Michele Yeo and Ginger A. Bertrand, for keeping me focused and organized. Having a hectic schedule with multiple projects on the go made it quite difficult to find the time to recipe test and write, but you guys did a great job of ensuring that I stayed the course and made it to the finish line. Thank you also to Jennifer Griffiths, the incredible designer and illustrator of this book; to Colin Rier; and everyone else at Penguin Random House Canada involved in publishing *Yawd*.

To the Fields brothers, Alex and AJ: you guys entered my life at a crucial time. Without your involvement in the Yawd pop-up it definitely wouldn't have made the impact it did on the Toronto dining scene. You guys have bright futures ahead of you, and I can't wait to see where your talents and tenacity take you.

To John Molina, my go-to photographer: this project was definitely a labor of love for us, years in the making. From being roommates to you shooting all my social media content, we've developed a chemistry and honed a specific style of art that we both can be proud of. Most people would think that shooting on a tropical island would be a photographer's dream, but we had all sorts of challenges—everything from sporadic rainfall and swarms of mosquitoes to dehydration from being in the sun all day. You took it all like a champ, and I am forever grateful for you being such a soldier and roughing it with me through it all.

To my dear Regina: you wore many hats in the production of this book—from recipe taster and hand model to food stylist and creative director, and, of course, designated driver. I wouldn't have been able to pull this off without your support, attention to detail, and inability to accept anything less than perfection when it comes to the overall brand identity of Yawd. Not to mention the hours of labor you dedicated to making our pop-ups a success before this cookbook was even an idea. Thank you for being the best partner in both business and life. I'm looking forward to making many more memorable moments with you!

And last but not least, I'd like to thank you. Yes, I'm actually talking to you; you have supported me over the last 12 years! Thank you for attending all my pop-ups since 2009; thank you for patronizing my restaurants; thank you for cheering me on through your TV screen. Thank you for every direct message, like, comment, and share; thank you for cooking my recipes and sharing them with your friends and family; thank you for all your continued support. I hope this cookbook makes you proud, and these recipes even become staples in your home—from my yawd to yours.

Index